HEALING
DEATH'S
WOUNDS

HEALING DEATH'S WOUNDS

HOW TO COMMIT THE DEAD TO GOD AND DELIVER THE OPPRESSED

MICHAEL MITTON & RUSS PARKER

Chosen
Grand Rapids, Michigan

© 2004 by Michael Mitton and Russ Parker

Published by Chosen Books
A division of Baker Publishing Group
P.O. Box 6287 Grand Rapids, MI 49516-6287
www.chosenbooks.com

Printed in the United States of America

Published in the U.K. by Arcadia Publishing Services Ltd, Reverie, Keels Hill, Peasdown St. John, Bath BA2 8EW.

This edition is a reworking of *Requiem Healing* by Michael Mitton and Russ Parker, originally published by Dartman, Longman and Todd in 1991.

Library of Congress Cataloging-in-Publication Data
Mitton, Michael.
    Healing death's wounds : how to commit the dead to God and deliver the oppressed / Michael Mitton and Russ Parker.
        p.   cm.
    Includes bibliographical references.
    ISBN 0-8007-9370-6 (pbk.)
    1. Prayers for the dead—Anglican Communion. I. Parker, Russ. II. Title.
BV227.M58 2004
265'.85—dc22   2004008662

We would like to dedicate this book
to Sarah and Paul,
and to Stanley and Turve,
who pray for us

Contents

[*]Written by Michael Mitton
[†]Written by Russ Parker
[‡]Written by both Michael Mitton and Russ Parker

7

Foreword

Should there be any communication between the land of the living and of the dead? Can the dead influence us, and do we need to be freed at times from that influence? Should we pray for the dead? Can houses be haunted?

These are very real questions, not only in movies but among people I know. Most Christians do not know how to answer, aside from some simple (and often simplistic) responses: "You're talking about superstitious nonsense" or "It's very real, but it's all demonic, so stay away from it."

Catholics have been somewhat open to these topics because of their tradition of purgatory. Yet in the past forty years, Catholics have heard less and less about the subjects of purgatory and praying for the dead.

In this clearly written and fascinating book, two evangelical authors, with open, inquiring minds but with a devotion to scriptural truth, courageously investigate all the main questions people ask. And not only ask, but actually encounter, such as, "Have you ever experienced the presence of some departed relative in your house? What are you supposed to do about it?"

This little book is honest and, I believe, the best answer from a Protestant, evangelical perspective to a crucial pastoral problem. The authors identify what is truly spiritually dangerous, especially in a world increasingly influenced by spiritualism—not only in movies and novels but in real life. At the same time they rescue what is valuable in the relationship between the living and the dead. What do we cut off and what do we preserve?

This is the kind of balanced presentation I think every well-educated Christian, and especially every pastor, should read.

Francis MacNutt, founding director
Christian Healing Ministries, Jacksonville, Florida

Introduction

The beginnings of this book happened a number of years ago in England when I, Michael Mitton, was serving as a curate at St. Andrew's Church, High Wycombe. It was not long after I had arrived that I went to one of our weekly clergy "team" meetings. High Wycombe was one parish with many Anglican churches working together.

One of the benefits of this arrangement was that clergy within each team, who were often of different backgrounds, met together regularly, sharing from the riches of our different traditions. I have to admit, though, to feeling rather put out on one occasion when the subject of the dead was being discussed. One of the team vicars present, who was from an Anglo-Catholic tradition, said that he could not imagine living this life without some reference to the faithful departed, to whom he prayed and from whom, he claimed, he received daily support as they prayed for him. Not only did he affirm this, he appeared to believe it passionately, and he was shocked to discover that I did not share his views!

My own background is evangelical and so this Catholic comment well and truly stuck in my Protestant throat. *He is wrong, of course,* I said to myself as I mused on this on the way home. Soon after this, I found myself assisting at another church in town that had an Anglo-Catholic tradition. It was a lively, loving church with a warm and happy heart. The vicar was Fr. John Hadley, who was held in great affection by his church, and whom I admired and trusted. Again, assisting at the Easter liturgy, I found myself confronted by this strange doctrine having to do with the dead. People seemed actually to *like* the dead, but not in a spiritualistic way; they seemed in their worship to have a very real sense of the fellowship of all believers who had died. I noticed that this was an important part of their faith.

I lived with this puzzle for some time. My main problems about this were threefold. Firstly, this type of acknowledgment of the dead seemed to me inexorably to lead into some type of spiritualism. Surely if you start talking about the dead, you will start communicating with them, and then you are on the slippery slope into spiritualism. Secondly, to start acknowledging the dead in worship takes you quickly into worshiping the dead—after all, it cannot be denied that in some parts of the world people seem to find it easier to have a personal relationship with the saints and worship them, than to have a relationship with Jesus and worship Him. Then, thirdly, I could not see how you could pray for the dead without diluting considerably the Gospel of salvation by faith alone. It seemed to stand to reason that once you start praying for the dead—such as praying for them to get through purgatory to heaven—you are thereby "assisting" Jesus with the work of salvation.

I imagine that many of us who come from an evangelical starting place in our pilgrimages face these objections. But somehow I could not just close the book and rest at ease. I was troubled by it in mind and spirit.

The more I thought about this, the more my theology seemed inadequate. It failed to come to my rescue at some important moments in my pastoral work. I remember going on a routine funeral visit and finding that the bereaved family had asked for the coffin, containing the deceased mother, to be in the house for 24 hours prior to the funeral. So here I was doing my funeral visit, and "Mum" was very much with us, resting in peace by the window.

The mourning husband asked rather meekly, "Would you say some prayers for her?" and we all moved round the coffin and looked on the gray, waxen face of the woman who had meant so much to that family. They still loved her, just as Mary loved Jesus and wanted to show her love and respect by visiting the tomb. This woman was not a churchgoer, but she may have had faith. I did not know her final destination. I could not pray for her salvation but I found I could pray a prayer entrusting her to God and expressing our love and sorrow to our Father in heaven. Something felt pastorally right about this and it was not inconsistent with my doctrinal objections outlined above.

I remember on another occasion praying with an elderly woman who was the mother of our churchwarden. She had not had a happy life but on her deathbed she made her peace with God. I was with her and her daughter moments after she died. It was one of those sacred moments—that time just after a death, when you know the person has gone and yet you feel rather like someone at a railway station watching the train disappear slowly into the distance. Our prayer was a sort of waving goodbye, praying for God to welcome her and to embrace her and heal her from all life's wounds. We knew He would do this anyway, of course, but we wanted to bless what He was going to do and, as any children would, we wanted to be sure He knew what we wanted.

During this time I came across Dr. Kenneth R. McAll's book, *Healing the Family Tree*.[1] Here was a man who identified with no particular wing of the Church: He was Pentecostal in some of his beliefs and Catholic in others. The book caused me to think further about the whole area of the activity of death. From this searching emerged my booklet *The Quick and the Dead*.[2] I was helped in the writing of that booklet by Russ Parker, and as we talked and discussed the subject together it seemed right to us to put our thoughts down in the form of this book.

We had no idea how people would react to this approach to healing the hurts of death. We were gratefully surprised to find that most people shared with us how they had found physical healing for themselves and personal release and healing for their families and children. As such it has confirmed for us the love and grace of God for us all and that His power reaches into wounds that sting us from beyond the grave.

This book, then, originally published under the title *Requiem Healing*, is by both of us. We have each taken separate chapters, as noted on the Contents page. Since the book was first published it has become much more popular for churches and cathedrals to hold services of remembrance around the time of All Saints' Day, November 1, as an opportunity to celebrate the lives of those who have died. Partially in response to this growing need we revised this book and included some new prayers for the healing of relationships between the living and those they grieve for and miss so much.

Dr. Kenneth McAll died in June 2001 and his passing reminds us of our debt to his insight and teaching. He founded Family Tree Ministries, and by the time of his death, his life's work had become more publicly accepted and respected. This must have given him much blessing and satisfaction. As part of the research for this book, we spent four hours in conversation with Dr. McAll, and we both look upon that occasion as one rich with surprises and stories of God's amazing grace.

Russ now writes about how he was drawn into this area.

In the autumn of 1975 a number of threads came together in my life that resulted in a new perspective on the issue of healing past hurts—especially when they related to an unplanned and painful death or unfinished bereavement. Before this time I had not properly considered the appropriateness of praying for the dead or the possibility that the living might still be affected by their dead relatives.

As an evangelical I considered the dead a closed book. They were either saints in glory or else awaiting judgment. In either case their situations were known only to God. There was to be no tampering in this area and no changes were to be expected now that they were dead. Like most Christians, I felt that the only constructive response to make in the face of death was thanksgiving and praise to God for those whose faith had enabled them to be taken home to be with their heavenly Father forever. Those who delved any further into this subject were decidedly suspect—either spiritualists or other trespassers into a forbidden spiritual zone. I was to gain some fresh insights into this whole area, however, and in the process discover something more of the healing ministry of the Lord Jesus Christ.

As a pastor I prayed with a number of parishioners who were coming to terms with the miscarriage of a first child. Each couple told me that the doctor had called and, in trying to comfort them, had explained that this unfortunate experience was quite normal and that it would not prevent them from having further children. Indeed for most this proved to be the truth.

What challenged me, however, was the anger that some of them felt when the doctor had tried to console them. The professional but detached manner of the general practitioner, they said, left them feeling belittled. They also objected to the doctor's use of the term *fetus* rather than *baby* because it seemed impersonal. In all they felt that their children were being depersonalized and that their grief was not being recognized.

Many of these parents, even though several years had elapsed, still felt stuck by the lack of closure surrounding the loss of that first child. Healing came only when they were given the opportunity to pray for the miscarried child and, for some, to name the child and commend him or her to God's merciful keeping.

I had gained this insight from a meeting with Dr. Kenneth McAll, a pioneer in this field. I first met him in 1975 when I was invited to speak at Foxhills, the Anglican diocesan center for the Chester diocese, on the basic principles of counseling and healing. I learned that the other speaker was to be Dr. McAll. I was told that he was a psychiatrist and a GP, among many other things.

In his talks Dr. McAll often focused on his experiences of counseling parents who had lost children through miscarriage or abortion. That information was not always known to him at the outset, however. When dealing with clients who were suffering either from depression or anxiety, and for which no apparent reason could be found, Dr. McAll would ask his patients if there had been other problems in the family's experience. Quite often this form of enquiry led to the admission that a child had been aborted or lost through a miscarriage. (On other occasions the problem seemed to relate to adults who had died without being prepared or who, in death, still carried unresolved burdens with them.)

Dr. McAll would then ask the parents if they had held a proper funeral service for their lost child and named him or her in faith before God. The usual response was one of surprise, for most of the parents had discounted the fetus as a real person. Dr. McAll then shared that in almost every case when the parents reclaimed their lost child, prayed for him, named him and even apologized for not owning him as a real child, the illness or trauma was healed.

Dr. McAll maintained that, in effect, what was happening was that the young children, in being rejected or ignored, had tried to signal their presence to living members of the family. Usually they chose someone who was receptive to them, and such people would in fact begin to feel the emotions of the dead child—feelings such as rejection, depression and a sense of lostness. He gave as an example the story of a young boy who, totally out of character, began to steal things from the local shops. He was a normal child who enjoyed the love and security of his home. Indeed, he gave away all the things he stole as he had no need for them.

His mother took him to the school counselor and to various consultants in an effort to understand his behavior, all to no avail. Eventually his mother shared her concern with Dr. McAll. In his usual manner he drew up a chart listing all the members of the family and then asked if there were any members who were now deceased. The answer was a partial no. When

Dr. McAll asked for clarification the woman said that some years before her son was born she had had an abortion. This child was duly prayed for and named in faith, and the mother apologized for what she had done. From that day onward her son ceased to steal from the shops!

As I listened to this and other case histories of healings, I was making a number of theological objections. Surely there is to be no contact between the living and the dead; did not the parable of the rich man and Lazarus make this clear? (See Luke 16:19–31.) Dr. McAll was implying that the dead affect the health of the living. Was he confusing the fact of demonic oppression with his idea of people being stuck in a sort of limbo state? And might not this way of thinking lead those who are sick to project their problems onto the dead and not take responsibility for their own lives?

And what about universalism? If the living, by recognizing the dead, can set them free from being trapped, then surely this implies the potential for salvation other than personal commitment to Jesus Christ as Lord and Savior. If so, then anybody recognized by the living, irrespective of his relationship to Jesus, could now enter heaven. As an evangelical I objected to what I was hearing.

In my heart, however, I simply started to cry. Whatever questions I was raising in my mind, I suddenly realized that Dr. McAll was helping parents connect with the grief they carried for children they had lost but for whom they had never mourned. Dr. McAll's talks helped me understand that no matter how physically incomplete such miscarried lives were, these were individuals made in the image of God just as much as I was. Such children may have been lost to their parents but never to God. It occurred to me that they had gone straight to be with the Lord and had in fact been growing up in heaven with their Father, the saints and the angels!

My immediate response was to get alone and pray about this. I soon realized that I had been given important insight on how to pray with people who had lost children through any early and unexpected death. When I put this insight into action, the results were amazing. Many people experienced a lifting of the depression that had hung over their lives for a long time. They found new hope. Many gave thanks to God for their children and said that they would be looking forward to meeting them when they went home to be with their heavenly Father. Many also expressed regret to God that they had not recognized these children as being real people and belonging to their families. Others felt deep peace inside and registered feelings of being a complete parent at last.

In reflecting on all of this, I can say that many I have prayed with have benefited from real inner healing concerning the loss of their children. Yet as a conservative evangelical, have I suddenly stepped onto a bypath meadow?

Now Michael continues.

Russ ends up asking the same question as I do. It came to me when I was discussing the question of journeys at a conference I was attending. I remember talking about this part of the journey and how it was for me as an evangelical. I said that it felt for me as if I were exploring a country road and had come across an interesting area of woodland that I wanted to investigate. The woodland represented the whole area that this book is discussing, which has to do with a Christian understanding of the dead. Around this wood, however, there was a substantial fence, and by this fence was placed a sign that read:

> WARNING!
> NO EVANGELICALS ALLOWED IN HERE.
> PROMINENT LEADERS HAVE EXPLORED
> THIS AREA AND FOUND IT TO BE
> DANGEROUS!
> GO NO FURTHER!

The awkward part of me wanted to know why I could not go further. And if it really was forbidden territory then I wanted to know why.

So as we now get into the book we invite you to explore with us. It is our conviction that, far from being a hostile and forbidden world, this woodland offers some surprising treasure: It will enrich our understanding of life and death; it will affect the way we pastor the bereaved, foster hope in the faithful, commit the dead to God and deliver the oppressed.

Michael Mitton and Russ Parker

1

Feelings for the Dead

When Pope John XXIII was told that he was going to die he remarked, "My bags are packed, I am ready to leave!"

Death has become, it seems, a topic of everyday conversation. This became true for many of us with the destruction of the World Trade Center in New York City on September 11, 2001. Terrorists loyal to Osama bin Laden flew jets into each of the giant twin towers and brought them thundering to the ground. Another jet exploded into the Pentagon outside Washington, D.C., and a fourth jet crashed short of its target, killing everyone on board.

The tremor shocks from these incidents, which killed nearly three thousand people, affected the whole world. Night after night news reports on television replayed scenes of disaster. Pictures of brave firemen, police officers and chaplains plunging into smoke-filled buildings in order to try and save lives gripped viewers for weeks on end. When this atrocity was linked to the Islamic fundamentalist network of al-Qa'eda, based within

Afghanistan and under the protection of the ruling faction, the Taliban, the shocked anger of the Western nations resulted in a bombing campaign that brought the Taliban party to its knees.

What emerged more closely to home was that church attendance began to rise noticeably as people were confronted with a massive onslaught to their sense of security and wellbeing. They needed reassurance that everything was going to be all right. They were also looking for healing from the shock and were trying to make sense of the seeming madness of the world.

We see parallel issues here when we think of the impact of the tragic death of Princess Diana in a car crash in Paris in 1997. The level of mourning was astounding as hundreds of thousands of people around the world grieved with us in Britain at her loss. The pavements outside Kensington and St. James Palaces in London were engulfed by an ocean of flowers, poetry and keepsakes, most given by people who had never met her. She was the icon of a suffering and innocent princess who had gone tragically early to her grave. Her life, though not without improprieties, had touched a nerve in the hopes and fears and aspirations of millions, and we grieved to see such youth and beauty scarred by the cruelties of the world.

The list could go on and on. In Great Britain in the 1980s, for instance, the subject of death was seldom out of the headlines. In the closing years of that decade an unprecedented number of tragic accidents took the lives of many hundreds of people.

It began in March 1987 with the sinking of the passenger ferryboat *Herald of Free Enterprise* and the deaths of 193 people. Millions watched television newsreels showing it going down in the English Channel. Gail Cook was one of the survivors and she spoke for many when she said:

> I still don't sleep properly. It all still runs through my mind and even when I do sleep I'm dreaming about it. . . . [I] dreamed of my friend on there the other night. He kept saying to me, 'I'm not dead, I'm still with you.' [1]

A few months later was the fire at King's Cross station in London. Thirty-one people perished in the flames. Then followed the explosion of the *Piper Alpha* platform in the North Sea claiming the lives of 167 men. Many were never found.

As the nation began to adjust to life after the *Piper Alpha* oil rig disaster, another series of appalling accidents took place within six months. The issue of death once again became immediate to the populace. Just before Christmas 1988, a Pan Am 747 jet was blown out of the sky by a terrorist bomb, killing all 270 passengers. The shattered plane scattered its debris over the Scottish town of Lockerbie, killing yet more people. In the same month a train collision at Clapham took the lives of 33 people.

Then as soon as the Christmas celebrations were over, in January 1989, a British Midland plane crash-landed on the M1 motorway near Kegworth in Derbyshire, claiming the lives of 46 people. I remember how deeply it affected many of the local clergymen who were called to pray with the dying and the dead. One in particular described how painful he found it to be in the fuselage of the broken aircraft among many who were crying and calling out for comfort. "It was like being in a communal grave," he said.

And in the following April, as if this were not enough tragedy to contemplate, 95 Liverpool football fans at the Hillsborough ground in Sheffield were crushed to death by a mob of thousands in an enclosure from which they could not escape. For the next few weeks thousands of people laid almost a quarter of a million wreaths on the playing field.

The final act in this spate of death was that of the Thames pleasure boat that was rammed one September night and sank quickly with the loss of 29 young lives.

The nation was reeling from one shock after another, and many of us will carry memories of the graphic scenes for the rest of our lives. For most of the world, these tragedies were viewed from a distance. In such cases, the grieving passes gradually as people return to their routines of life. When death touches us personally, however, the process of bereavement is not so easily dismissed.

I remember inviting a retired GP to give a series of talks at a Christian counseling course on the subject of bereavement. As she spoke she suddenly stopped and began to cry. She quickly composed herself and apologized, saying that she still missed her husband enormously. He had died more than ten years earlier. Her candor actually helped others to begin sharing some of their own unfinished grieving, and it became a valuable time of learning for all concerned. The sense of loss can be powerful and can affect people in different ways.

The term *bereavement* comes from the word *reave*, which means "to ravage, rob and leave desolate." It is no small wonder, then, that grieving persons can feel depressed, anxious, hostile and hysterical. There may be frequent bouts of physical pain and total weakness. Others may feel numb or find difficulty sleeping or controlling their bowel movements. Sometimes the feelings are locked inside until something happens to trigger them and the grief comes bursting out in tears and cries. Actually, this is quite beneficial. It is rather as if an underground stream, having been blocked by a fallen rock, is now free of its obstruction and can flow normally.

It is important to realize that grieving is a normal and healthy process that must not be hurried through. At the end of this journey is healing, a coming to terms with life and loss, and movement on into the future. As Christians we must take to heart the fact that it is those who do actually mourn whom Christ will bless and comfort (see Matthew 5:4). It is precisely for these reasons that a period of ritual mourning is important; it helps to underline that there has been a loss and that one has to go on from this point.

John Hinton makes this point well when he says:

> The practice of mourning provides more than this socially approved catharsis of grief. It insists that the death has occurred, repeatedly demonstrating this fact over a few days so that the bereaved, whatever their state of mind, accept the painful

knowledge, assimilate it and begin to plan accordingly. Viewing the body and taking part in the funeral emphasises beyond all doubt that the person is really dead. The condolences, the discussion of the deceased in the past tense, the newspaper announcements, the public recognition of the death, all affirm the loss.[2]

There are, however, many people who get stuck in their grieving, who cannot or will not make the mourner's journey to wholeness. Consider, for example, the stark contrast in response to the death of a son in the lives of two radically different individuals: the Ayatollah Khomeini and "Daddy" King, the father of Martin Luther King Jr. The Ayatollah's hatred for the Shah of Iran and his American supporters began when his son was executed by the Shah. From his unresolved grief came the desire for revenge, which eventually caused an international crisis and entangled the whole Middle East in a conflict that is still unresolved. Daddy King's grief for his son took a different route and led to peace rather than war. After Martin Luther King was murdered, the King family gathered together and resolved that Martin's vision of peace would die with him unless they forgave the murderer. Together they grieved for Martin; they cried until they came to the place where they could pray and forgive. Because of their process of grieving they were enabled to move forward in their lives and carry on their work.

Elisabeth Kübler-Ross, in her well-known book *On Death and Dying*,[3] says that the first identifiable response to the subject of death is denial. The individual pushes the subject of death away because it is too threatening and disturbing. In an attempt to maintain balance in life, the one who is dying or grieving a loss denies that there is a death to be faced or overcome. In time the denial moves through the process of anger, bargaining, depression and then finally acceptance. Another way of summarizing this procedure is to say that mourning helps us to move from still holding on to the dead to letting go of the dead. We shall now explore some of the reasons why people hold on to their dead.

HOLDING ON TO THE DEAD

For many the adjustment to accepting the finality of death and separation takes time. There are many examples of the bereaved sensing the dead as still "being there" with them. This may go as far as feeling the touch of the loved one's arm or hearing her voice speak comforting words or give guidance. Others report smelling the tobacco of his familiar pipe or seeing her walking down the street or sitting in a favorite armchair.

It must be stated that for many this brings great comfort, and as Christians we must be sensitive not to demolish such feelings in our haste to be theologically accurate and defensive. As we will find later in our study, these experiences can indeed signal a connection of sorts with our deceased loved ones. But there are other explanations as well. For some, the bereavement is so intolerable that the unconscious mind refuses to believe that a death has happened. It manufactures this kind of phenomenon in an attempt to convince the conscious mind that the loved one is still alive and present. In the course of this book we will explore the area of discernment and learn to test the validity of these and other experiences. If it is a case of manufacturing a manifestation, counselors can usually help the bereaved person come to terms with the reality of the death and let go.

Another reason why some people hold on to their dead is because they believe that they are silent companions or guides for the living. Alan Billings points out the folk culture in a lot of people's understanding of death when he quotes the following from the obituary columns of the *Leicester Mercury*:

> Those we love don't go away
> They walk beside us every day
> Unseen, unheard, but always near
> Still loved, still missed, still very dear.[4]

He goes on to say that such verses are not necessarily evidence of religious faith but examples of how religious imagery is all that is available to nominal believers for expressing their thoughts and feelings. It is here that the minister must be careful not to collude with such fantasies while seeking to support the hurting. The reality of death and the separation it brings must not be denied. Billings encourages the Christian in pastoral care to avoid using terms such as *falling asleep*, which, though mentioned in the Bible, may dull the sharp reality of death. As Christians we need to help these people recognize that their loved ones are now with God, who is all just, and in their mourning leave them in His capable hands.

Another reason why people hold on to their dead is because they are told that the dead wish to hold on to them. Some years ago I was speaking to a self-help bereavement group in Leicester. One of the elderly widowers in that group came up to me and said that he had been contacted by members of a local spiritualist church. They relayed that in one of their meetings a medium had received a communication from his wife, who had died some six weeks earlier. If he would care to come to one of their meetings he would hear for himself what his wife wished to say to him. This he duly did, and now he lived for the moments he could go to the meetings in the hope of hearing from his former partner.

I could not help feeling angry and sad at the same time: angry because he was getting involved in something that is clearly opposed to the Christian message, namely, trying to contact the dead (see Deuteronomy 18:10–12); sad because he still seemed unhappy and, because of his frequent and often forlorn visits to the meetings, was not being allowed to go through the process of grieving, which would have led him to a more wholesome approach to life and death.

We must admit that there has indeed been a revival of interest in the world of psychic phenomena, spiritualism and wizardry. The breathtaking success of the Harry Potter books and the films of the same name demonstrates the renewed enthusiasm among young and old alike for all things magical. Many of us remember the publicity when Shirley MacLaine endorsed her spirit guide and Linda Evans revealed that she has followed guidance from a discarnate entity named Mafu. British television programs show how certain people have tried to contact the dead, and American TV commercials broadcast "psychic hotline" numbers.

Further interest in holding on to the dead is aroused by claims that the dead continue their life's work through the living. A program on BBC2 television a number of years ago was called "Spirits from the Past." On one show renowned pianist John Lill claimed that the composer Beethoven was enabling him to play better by communicating part of his mind to the pianist. Such claims abound and many are being given consideration. Recently the London Symphony Orchestra, together with the Ambrose Singers, performed a sacred oratorio called "Beyond the Veil," which was allegedly composed by Handel and communicated by the dead composer to a spiritualist teacher.

Most of this modern fascination with the dead was propelled by the New Age movement, which made its appearance about fifty years ago. The Christian Gospel proclaims that beyond the fact of death there is a resurrection life to be experienced through our Lord Jesus Christ; New Agers seemingly deny the fact and content of death. Humanist psychologist Maxine Negri explains their belief that all human goals are possible, including breaching the dividing wall of death. This is done through one's own human, independently earned, spiritual enlightenment.[5] This means that the living have the ability to tap into the life essence or spirit of the departed and so remain in contact.

In the next chapter we shall examine much more closely what the Bible has to say about contact with the departed, but suffice it to say here that such interest in alleged contacts creates confusion as to just which frontiers actually separate the living and the dead. The matter is made more complex by two further areas of reported contact with the dead—that of clinical or near-death experiences and the healing that many claim to have received by praying for the sins and needs of departed ancestors.

Dr. Raymond Moody, in his book *Life After Life*,[6] wrote about the stories patients related to him when they had had near-death experiences. The dying man may have heard his doctor pronounce him dead, while at the same time he may have felt as if his body were being sucked rapidly through a long tunnel where he seemed to approach a "being of light." Relatives and friends who had died would come forward and help bring him toward the light. All this would be accompanied by feelings of great acceptance and warmth and a complete absence of judgment. The majority of those who return from such encounters say that they are now more determined to live fuller and better lives, and this often includes some form of religious commitment.

A lot of research has gone into this phenomenon and, while little credence is given to the stories as actual encounters of a person who has died, evidence shows nonetheless that they are healing experiences.

Such accounts raise a number of questions as far as conservative evangelical belief is concerned. Do these stories mean, for example, that there is no accounting for personal sin and that there is no need to repent and be born again? Such testimonies of non-judgmentalism and acceptance for all, irrespective of whether the person was a practicing Christian or not, surely imply universalism, in which there is no need for conversion and embracing the Gospel of salvation. Matthew and Dennis Linn shrug off this concern by saying that people are far more likely to be motivated to faith and Christian living by the image of a loving and forgiving father than by a vindictive and judgmental father.[7] They support their statement by referring to the Prodigal Son who never found his restored place in the family until he received the embrace of his accepting and loving father. Then came confession and new life (see Luke 15:11–32). This is, however, an oversimplification of the story. It overlooks the fact that the son first underwent a period of conviction and repentance before returning to his father's embrace.

I do not think that it is suitable to use these "near-death" experiences as a means to formulate beliefs about the nature of salvation or the alleged absence of judgment. Neither do I think that such encounters are demonic in origin simply because of the implications of universalism and the absence of reference to the unique salvation offered through Jesus Christ. What is quite obvious is that the patients do not die but recover. We do not have, therefore, the finality of death and subsequent salvation without the need of conversion. What we do have is an awareness that God, the Supreme Being, is by nature loving and forgiving. This is good news for the fallen, and those who do recover seem to go on with greater openness to God in their lives.

While this is not generally a salvation experience, it does at least give a better opportunity for the individual to respond to the Gospel at a later date. We must note that many people who have been resuscitated have also been confronted with their sinfulness. Dr. Maurice Rawlings, who worked for many years in the resuscitation unit of a large hospital in Chicago, describes how he prayed with one such person who accepted Jesus' atoning death and who went on to live a committed Christian life.[8]

The appearance of dead friends and relatives in some of the stories quoted in *Life After Life* does not suggest necessarily that such departed were automatically saved after death when they were known to have rejected Christ when they were alive. After all, we are not certain if these people are actually there or are just a part of the person's unconscious thinking. So all we can state confidently on this matter at the moment is that, for the person concerned, such deceased are important for differing reasons.

The traditional evangelical teaching on relationships between the living and the dead is that there is to be no contact at all. Richard Bewes says that the biblical revelation does not seem to encourage the merging of this world and the next. If we try to do this, several errors begin to raise their heads: "sentimentalism . . . sensationalism, where discipleship can become diverted and blunted . . . and spiritualism."[9] Yet we do believe as Christians that these two worlds will merge at the glorious reunion of all the dead in Christ and those still alive on the earth on the day when Jesus Christ returns in power and glory (see 1 Thessalonians 4:15–18). Any crossing of the boundaries between the living and the dead before this event is regarded with the deepest suspicion.

The kinds of sightings we have just been discussing are regarded, therefore, as entirely subjective in nature, and we are well advised not to dwell upon such experiences. While the perspective of this book is not to encourage any seeking after the dead or involvement with spiritism, we nonetheless recognize that for many people such near-death encounters do produce a less anxious approach to death. We would also acknowledge the need in us to cherish and continue to love those who have died. This we believe does not conflict with evangelical belief.

Some Christians believe that such events should be accepted as part of God's providence and received as encouragement to live more positively and look toward life eternal with more determined peace of heart. This approach is conveyed by Jean Darnell as recorded in her autobiography, *Heaven Here I Come*. Jean relates how she and her mother were converted to Christ through an evangelistic mission when she was about nine years old. Not long after this time her mother had a serious illness and died. A registered nurse on the scene pronounced her dead. Both Jean and her father were stunned by this sudden death. Jean cried and cried and prayed that Jesus would give her mother back to them. While she was crying and praying, her mother "came back to life."

The story that unfolded from her mother was not dissimilar to those told by Moody and Rawlings, save for the fact that Jean's mother recognized her own mother, who came and escorted her to a lovely garden. She was sure it was her mother even though she had never met her, for she had died three days after giving birth. While there in the garden she heard Jesus telling her that her spirit was to return to earth because her daughter was crying for her so much. What also makes this story interesting is that, at a later date, Jean's mother visited her own mother's eldest sister in West Virginia and was shown an old photograph of a group of people. She instantly pointed out her own mother and said that she was the woman whom she had met in heaven. Apparently this was the only photograph of Jean's grandmother, and neither Jean nor her mother had ever seen it.[10]

So near-death encounters with the dead, while not strictly provable, do not really infringe upon our basic belief that we are to leave the dead in the hands of God. Meetings such as these were not deliberately sought after, and they do suggest that there may be some area of legitimate encounter with the departed. At the very least these stories convey to us that our departed are still important to us, and this fact should not be minimized or denied.

PRAYING FOR THE DEPARTED

The second area of contact with the dead in this discussion is that of prayer for the departed as it relates to their alleged influence on the living. This does not necessarily involve the sighting of the deceased. It suggests, rather, that the issues that concerned some deceased relatives are in some way being visited upon the living. There is certainly a great deal of evidence in the Bible that the sins of the parents can indeed be brought upon their descendants and for a number of generations. The most often quoted reference in the Bible to this phenomenon is this: "I, the LORD your God, am a jealous God, punishing the children for the sin of the fathers to the third and fourth generation of those who hate me, but showing love to a thousand generations of those who love me and keep my commandments" (Exodus 20:5–6; Deuteronomy 5:9–10; see also Numbers14:18). In addition are verses stating that the sins of the parents will take the effect of curses being visited upon the children who shall come afterward. Such generational effects are diseases, disasters and lingering illnesses (see Deuteronomy 28:59; see also 28:18, 32; 30:1–2, 19).

This idea is countered by scholars who refer to the fact that God has made a new covenant by which the individual is now accountable only for his own sins. God speaks to Ezekiel, for example, about the proverb: "The fathers eat sour grapes, and the children's teeth are set on edge" (Ezekiel 18:2). He goes on to say that from then on the salvation of individuals will be attributed to their own choices and not that of their parents (see Ezekiel 18:3–32).

Still it is a matter of observation that often the twists and scars of our parents' experiences are carried on within the family, because the children are indeed shaped by the parents' approach to life. I know in my own case that I grew up in a family where sons and fathers did not get on well with each other. This puzzled me at first because I tried very hard to get close to my father but with little or no success. Then some years later, as I pursued my hobby of family history, I discovered that my father hardly knew my grandfather because the latter was quite withdrawn. My grandfather in turn could not get on with his father, a policeman, because he, too, was a remote figure who was hardly ever at home. My great-grandfather had to leave home to work when he was young, and soon afterward his father died.

I was able to trace a pattern of behavior down through generations of fathers and sons. The chain was broken only when I recognized what was happening and through prayer asked God to break the cycle in my life by giving me a capacity to love as a father and be loved as a person. I am happy to report that, although I have not succeeded in getting a lot further with my own father, my son and I do enjoy a loving relationship.

An extension of this syndrome is the belief that not only have the problematic issues of the parents been passed down to their children, but that the parents or ancestors themselves have somehow maintained a hold over their offspring. In this case the form of ministry that is usually recommended is prayer recognizing the deceased in question and acceptance before God of the consequential impact of their sins. It is often carried out in the form of a Communion service. This is a practice that has long been recognized in Roman Catholic and Anglo-Catholic churches; the evangelical Christian has rejected it, however, because it seems to undermine belief in the finality of death and judgment. Since it seems to be offering another chance for salvation to the deceased, it implies that the ministry of the Church at prayer is more effective than that of the atoning death of Jesus upon the cross. We shall look at this very closely when we examine the work of Dr. Kenneth McAll, the foremost practitioner of this form of healing, in a later chapter.

Perhaps the most well-known form in which this ministry is presented is that of dealing with ghosts and hauntings. Those who suffer from such appearances say they are convinced that a real person is bothering them. On January 16, 1990, I took part in a television program called "The Time, the Place." Of the many who shared their stories I recall one woman in particular. Joy talked about waking up in her bedroom to find a man leaning over her and almost smothering her. No words were exchanged but she was convinced that this "person" was in some way asking for help.

The question of the Christian is, What is the appropriate response to this kind of event? Whether we are dealing with the subjective life of the person telling the story, the demonic or the "unquiet dead," we need to recognize that we are at least handling the subject of how the living feel about the dead. We must accept such feelings, therefore, and be sensitive about how we proceed. We also need to recognize that in our ministry to the ones in need—whether they are facing bereavement, a haunting of some kind or some personal attachment to the departed—we must bring them to the place where they learn to free the dead.

FREEING THE DEAD

Dying has become a more remote part of our lives . . . when death occurs there is a fair chance that someone else [not a member of the family] will be the witness and that the care that precedes it will be done by others. So the language of death is foreign to us.[11]

Before we can help free those who have problems related to the dead we must enable them to come to terms with dying itself. We are still not as comfortable with the subject of death as were our Victorian ancestors, for whom it was an all too common event. It was no surprise for there to be at least one or two infant deaths in an average household. Grieving, tears and talking about the dead were familiar features of public and family life. Even in Christian circles there is still difficulty balancing feelings of grief with a robust belief in resurrection and eternal life.

I remember two funerals in particular that represented for me a closed and an open approach to grieving for the Christian. The first was upon the occasion of the death of a college principal's wife who was about seventy years old. As the cortege processed into the church, the widower walked behind the coffin, and although the congregation was singing a song of triumph, he looked sad and his face was quite pale. I overheard someone a few rows behind me say, "Look at him! He should be praising, not looking so sad and unbelieving." It seemed that the person could not equate pain and sadness with hope and faith in bereavement. For that person the husband should have been triumphant and not showing or perhaps feeling the sense of loss. How intolerant we Christians can be when another is hurting! Even Jesus wept at a funeral, and He is the Resurrection and the Life!

The second funeral took place in Richmond Baptist Church in Liverpool. This time it was the death of a young mother whose husband was a minister. The cortege entered the church with the husband and their five-year-old daughter walking side by side. The address was given by the widower who began his talk by saying, "I don't know why God let my wife suffer so much pain and die as she did in that car crash. I wish I did. I don't know why He let us move [to a new] house only to have Ann die three months later. I don't know why." You can imagine how emotional everyone was feeling by now. Then he went on to say, "But I do know this, that Jesus died for us all and rose again. That Jesus has promised eternal life to all those who trust in Him. And what I do know helps me to live with what I don't know." Here was hurt and hope being given equal expression.

It is this voicing of feeling and faith that brings balance into the journey of dying and that gives us a better opportunity to let go of the dead and learn to free them into God's hands. Otherwise, we will desire to hold on to them even after death. And there is also some room to conclude that the dead, because they were not properly prepared for death, try to hold on to the living.

While this is not a book about bereavement care and counsel, we feel nonetheless that it is important to encourage people to approach the issue of death in as whole and caring a fashion as possible. It is this letting go at dying and death that prevents any unhealthy holding on. It will also give us a better understanding when we meet people who say that they are still in contact with those who have died. We may well discover that the continued relationship with the departed exists because there is some form of unfinished business that concerned either the deceased or the living relative that has not yet been brought under the healing power of the Lord Jesus Christ.

Sheila Cassidy, in her book *Sharing the Darkness*, says of caring for the dying, that "it is here that we must learn the spirituality of the foot of the cross, the stance of the impotent bystander."[12] She goes on to list three basic attributes that we need in order to accompany the dying. First is an intensely down-to-earth practicality that does not flinch from the impact of the disintegration of human bodies and minds. Second is a much-needed sense of humor, for issues of life and death carry moments of tragi-comedy. Finally is the need for special sensitivity, a vulnerability to the pain of others that is often, but not always, the result of personal suffering.

These are the same qualities we need when we share with those who have continued a relationship with the departed.

They need to go on the journey the dying take, where the living learn to let go and free the one they love. It is not enough to sound out the dangers of spiritualism and possible deception. We need to uncover the issues that prevent the living from letting go of their dead and, in Jesus' name, direct His healing peace into their lives.

So far we have been saying that the living have all kinds of feelings about the dead and dying, which to some degree accounts for the way the living sustain a relationship with those who have died. This being the case, we have discussed the need for such people to let go of their dying and dead and so enter into an appropriate relationship with their departed. Here we recognize a general failing, particularly among evangelicals, to accept any kind of relating between the living and the departed. The very fact that we treasure the memory of our loved ones in our hearts means that we are still saying to them, "I love you and recognize your right to life." Let us, then, examine carefully to see if there are any relationships between the living and the dead that the Bible allows and that may be open to us, the living.

> Dear Master, all the flowers are Thine,
> And false the whisper, 'ours' and 'mine';
> We lift our hearts to Thee and say,
> 'Lord, it was Thine to take away'.
>
> And yet, though we would have it so,
> Lord, it is very good to know
> That Thou art feeling our pain
> And we shall have our flower again.
>
> So help us now to be content
> To take the sorrow Thou hast sent.
> Dear Lord, how fair Thy house must be
> With all the flowers we've lent to Thee![13]

2

Meeting with the Dead

A Biblical Survey

Jesus has forced open a door that has been locked since the death of the first man. He has met, fought, and beaten the king of death. Everything is different because He has done so.

C. S. Lewis

It is a basic Christian belief that God has access to the world of the living as well as the dead. Jesus underlined this truth when He said that His Father was not the God of the dead but of the living (see Matthew 22:32).[1] What makes this statement so startling is that Jesus had just been referring to the patriarchs, Abraham, Isaac and Jacob, who had been dead for centuries! They are obviously not dead to God but ever live before Him. This also suggests quite strongly that the dead have an ongoing relationship with God. The Scriptures give us some glimpses into the nature of this relationship. The Old Testament gives many references to the dead being like shadows of their former selves and inhabiting the world of "Sheol."[2]

Here they dwell in darkness and silence.[3] Great and humble alike live side by side in pale equality. Both Isaiah and Ezekiel write of God addressing the proud rulers of the nations as they come down into Sheol. We are told that even the dead are roused to speak to these men and remind them of how they have been reduced from their former glory.[4] This shadowy state of existence, however, is essentially something that the dead long to be freed from into a fuller life in the presence of God. David represents this hope when he says:

> You will not abandon me to the grave,
> nor will you let your Holy One see decay.
> You have made known to me the path of life;
> you will fill me with joy in your presence,
> with eternal pleasures at your right hand.
>
> Psalm 16:10–11[5]

The New Testament gives stronger indication that there is some sort of conscious awareness for the dead in the interval between death and resurrection. Before we look at these references we need to say something about "soul sleep." In a number of places the dead are referred to as those who sleep. Paul, seeking to encourage the Thessalonian church to hold on to their belief in the resurrection and to look forward to restored relationships with the dead, says to them:

> We do not want you to be ignorant about those who fall asleep, or to grieve like the rest of men, who have no hope. We believe that Jesus died and rose again and so we believe that God will bring with Jesus those who have fallen asleep in him.
>
> 1 Thessalonians 4:13–14[6]

This has largely been assumed to mean that the dead have no conscious awareness of their state and only awaken at the resurrection time. This interpretation, however, both misses the purpose of the metaphor and misunderstands the nature of dreaming itself. First, the purpose of the metaphor of sleep is to say that the individuals have not ceased to exist because they have died and been buried. For them life goes on even if we cannot relate to them as we would to any normal waking person. They sleep only in so far as we can perceive their state of existence, but this does not mean that they are not awake to the reality of being in the eternal presence of God. Second, although this was probably not Paul's uppermost thought in the use of this term, sleep is now known to be a highly active experience for the sleeper, whose mind and awareness are in fact in constant use.

Let us now turn to the imagery that suggests an ongoing and developing relationship with God for those who have died and who await their resurrection day when they shall be reunited with all the faithful in Christ. We find that many of these glimpses are given by Jesus Himself in His teaching.

JESUS' ONGOING RELATIONSHIP WITH THE DEAD

In the fourth gospel, Jesus speaks of dying in terms of going to the Father's house in which are many rooms (see John 14:2). Author B. F. Westcott points out that we must not be misled into thinking of modern, Western-style rooms, but rather that of a resting place or station on a great road where travelers find refreshment.[7] Archbishop William Temple says the word used here means a wayside *caravanserai*, which was akin to a motel for the camel caravans that crossed the great expanses of the ancient world. Such travelers would send a dragoman on ahead to prepare for the arrival of the caravan. Then, at night, when all the guests had arrived and the animals had been cared for, a friendly and convivial spirit prevailed. So Jesus presents Himself as our dragoman who has gone on ahead to prepare a resting place on the journey to the final destination.[8]

Temple draws out this theme of the resting place and under-lines the idea that in this case it is not the final destination for the Christian. It is indeed fellowship with Christ, fuller than before, but it is a stage on the journey as we press on to "the goal of the call upward which God gives in Christ Jesus."[9] It is quite conceivable then that the time the dead spend with Jesus before the resurrection and the reaching of our final destina-tion in God is spent in the Father's resting place where we are refreshed and renewed.

When Jesus was dying on the cross He turned to the penitent thief and said that on that very day they would both walk in paradise (see Luke 23:43). Commentator J. Norval Geldenhuys says that this passage is in complete agreement with the rest of the New Testament, which clearly teaches that immediately after death the saved associate spiritually with Jesus in heavenly bliss.[10] We might assume that the dead progress and mature in their faith because of this association with Jesus. This is certainly the burning desire of the apostle Paul when he says how he longs to depart and be with Christ.[11] The writer of the Hebrews seems to affirm this idea when he speaks of the "spirits of righteous men made perfect" (Hebrews 12:23).

This relationship between Jesus and the faithful dead also includes their sharing of hurt feelings and longings. John in his vision sees the martyrs of God calling out for the time of judgment to come (see Revelation 6:9–11). Granted, this is poetic vision; it nonetheless affirms the New Testament teach-ing of continuing relationships between God and the dead. It also suggests to us that the dead are aware of events upon the earth. This is further affirmed by references to the prayers of the saints in heaven (see Revelation 5:8–14; 8:3–5). On both occasions the prayers are of an intercessory nature because God answers their requests by a display of power and out-poured judgment on the earth. Of course the model for this continuation of prayer for others is Jesus Himself who, we are told, "always lives to intercede" for "those who come to God through him" (Hebrews 7:25).

What, then, do we conclude from this evidence? <u>Those who die in the faith of Christ go on developing in their faith and relationship with Jesus.</u> It seems as well that they are <u>aware to some degree of events among the living as their prayer life suggests.</u> I do not think that we are stretching the evidence to say that this process of continued growth is also true of children and babies who have died. Indeed, a cursory gleaning of the gospels will give us an insight into the special care that Jesus had for children, who, He said, would populate heaven (see Matthew 18:1–11). Personally I find it extremely attractive to think of all the young whose lives were terminated so tragically receiving an education in the company of Jesus and the angels!

What we now need to ask—if, indeed, there is such a state of awareness among the dead—is this: Is there a legitimate way in which the living and the dead can either relate to or affect each other? Certainly there is a strong message running throughout the Bible that forbids such practices as spiritualism, witchcraft and contacting the dead. The classic Old Testament passage for this is Deuteronomy 18:10–11: "Let no one be found among you who . . . practices divination or sorcery . . . engages in witchcraft, or casts spells, or who is a medium or spiritist or who consults the dead." The penalty for engagement in any of these practices was death.[12]

In the New Testament we are told of further punishment: Those who practice the occult (looking into things that God has hidden from us) will not inherit the Kingdom of God (see Galatians 5:19–21). Very often the parable of the rich man and Lazarus is used to underline this fact (see Luke 16:19–31). In this story Abraham speaks to the man in torment in the underworld. He says that it is not possible for the dead to return to life to warn the living, and that a gulf has in fact been fixed in the underworld between the righteous and the damned. Most commentators, however, say that this parable was not told to give details of the intermediate state of existence but rather to encourage the living to live by God's Word. In any event, we can conclude that, for the Christian, seeking to establish contact with the dead is forbidden. This does not mean that when someone dear to us dies we work hard at forgetting him and not enjoying our memories of him. To a large degree, other people become a part of us, and the deposit of what they have given us goes on enriching our lives.

Along with the parables Jesus told, we find that God has given us in Scripture a record of actual contacts between the living and the dead. Most of these are taken from the New Testament. This should be no surprise to us when we consider that Jesus describes Himself as the Resurrection and the Life. An examination of these events will help us come to some knowledge of the relationship God Himself has created between the living and the dead.

SAUL AND THE MEDIUM OF ENDOR

The background to this account, which is given in 1 Samuel 28:3–25 and 1 Chronicles 10:13–14, is that of the imminent defeat of the Israelite army at the hands of the Philistines. King Saul has been trying desperately to get a prophetic word from God, but nothing seems to be working out. The aged prophet Samuel is now dead and so there is a lack of the prophetic guidance to which Saul has been accustomed. In desperation Saul goes in disguise to consult a medium at Endor. He asks that Samuel be brought up to him, presumably because he wants a word of guidance even from beyond the grave.

It is what happens next that has caused much debate. According to the context it is apparent that the real Samuel appears (see 1 Samuel 28:12–15). Saul recognizes the description given of the spirit, and Samuel seems to be disturbed by the events as well. Further indication that it is the real Samuel is that the medium recognizes him. She realizes then that the one making the inquiry is none other than Saul, who has forbidden such practices, and so she fears for her life. If we take the story at its face value it now seems that a formal mediumistic procedure is abandoned as Samuel and Saul engage in direct conversation. Samuel utters a terrible prophecy of doom for the house of Saul and says that he and his sons will soon be joining him in the world of the dead. Judging from Saul's reaction to this encounter, he is convinced he is meeting the real Samuel.

Dr. H. L. Wilmington outlines the various possibilities regarding whether this was the real Samuel or not:

1. *The appearance of Samuel was a psychological impression.*

   According to this view, the woman permitted herself to become emotionally involved. Thus she identified psychologically with the prophet Samuel and convinced herself that she had actually seen Samuel when she called him up. Alexander Maclaren sounds a similar chord when he says that it matters not whether the woman brought up Samuel or whether she was as much awed as Saul was by the coming up of an old man covered with the well-known mantle; it is the prophecy of doom that we should take note of.[13]

   There are two objections to this viewpoint. The medium cried out and was startled by the appearance of Samuel. Such would not be the case if she was identifying psychologically with the occasion. Second, as we have already noticed, Saul himself talked with Samuel; the normal procedure would have been for the medium to convey the message to the client.

2. *This was a demonic impersonation of Samuel.*

   Those holding this view suggest that whatever the outward form of the manifestation, it was but an impersonation of the real person. The defense for this approach is that God would not permit a woman involved in the occult to disturb the rest of a godly man nor use her to convey the word of the Lord. After all, Satan can appear as an angel of light (see 2 Corinthians 11:14).

   It is indeed true that many spiritistic phenomena are due to demonic spirits rather than to trickery or the psychic ability of the individual. This case, however, does not appear to be demonic. First, God has used some rather unclean characters to convey His word to others on a number of occasions. Consider the testimony of the prostitute Rahab who witnessed the word of the Lord to the spies she hid in her house (see Joshua 2:8–11). Then there is the example of the high priest Caiaphas who prophesied the death of Jesus for the Jewish nation, and he himself was implacably opposed to Jesus' ministry (see John 11:49–53).

It also seems doubtful that a demonic impersonation would have contained such a rebuke to Saul and a reminder to do properly the will of God. If anything, it was Saul himself who was afflicted by demonic spirits as his attempts to kill David and Jonathan testify.[14]

3. *This was a fake mediumistic encounter.*
   This view is sustained only if we accept that the woman alone saw Samuel and that Saul heard and saw nothing. This hardly fits the evidence of Scripture. It is also highly improbable that the woman would have given such a word of doom to the king when her own life might well be forfeited as a result.

4. *This was the real Samuel.*
   Wilmington says that this is the most popular view and it is the only one that fits all the evidence of the account.[15] What, then, is the purpose of God bringing the dead Samuel back to talk with the living Saul? Its purpose seems to be to emphasize the doom of Saul and God's displeasure at this attempt to contact the dead through a medium. John J. Davis notes that this is a completely unique event in the Bible and is not to be compared with the Transfiguration encounter of Elijah and Moses with Jesus, because they appeared in glory while Samuel was clad in his old prophet's mantle.[16]

So we have here contact between the dead and the living, which God Himself has commissioned for His own purposes. While this does not give us a mandate to expect regular occurrences of the same, it does at least establish that God, for His own sovereign will, can arrange an encounter between the living and the dead. It also illustrates for us that the words of the deceased can exert a powerful influence upon the living. Yet we must be quick to emphasize that this occurred only within the boundaries of God's word and express will.

THE TRANSFIGURATION OF JESUS

Whatever the glory and splendor of this moment on the mountain with the transfigured Jesus, Peter is quite convinced that at least two of the Old Testament saints have come back to life. In the story, told in Matthew 17:1–9, Mark 9:2–13 and Luke 9:28–36, he is sure that Elijah and Moses are not phantoms or elements of some vision he is having. He offers to build tents or booths for all three so that the moment can be prolonged by a time of rest and shelter. Although Jesus does not contradict Peter's confession that "it is good for us to be here" (Matthew 17:4), He nonetheless does not allow the encounter to become permanent. Indeed God's words, "This is my Son, whom I love. Listen to him!" (Mark 9:7), suggest that whatever the importance of the occasion, it must not overshadow our commitment to Jesus Christ as Lord.

There has been much speculation as to why these two people appear to Jesus. The Lucan narrative says that they inquire concerning Jesus' departure, or death and resurrection, in Jerusalem. Some scholars see this event as a parallel to the deliverance gained by the exodus from Egypt to the land of promise. J. C. Ryle says there can be little question that there is one main objective of this wonderful experience. It is meant to encourage the disciples by giving them a glimpse of good things yet to come.[17] Maclaren says that Moses and Elijah

are witnesses of an immortal life and proofs that his [Jesus'] yet unpierced hands held the keys of life and death. He opened the gate which moves backwards to no hand but his and summoned them; and they come, with no napkins about their heads and no trailing grave clothes entangling their feet, and own him as King of life. . . . Now these two are brought from hopeful repose,

perchance to learn how near their deliverance was; and behind
them we seem to discern a dim crowd of holy men and women
. . . who throng the portals of the unseen world, waiting for the
near advent of the better Samson to bear away the gates to the
city on the hill and lead thither their ransomed train.[18]

It seems quite logical that between them Moses and Elijah
speak of the Law and the prophetic word, both of which are
come to completion in Jesus Christ. Others have attempted to
see further significance in Moses and Elijah. H. A. Ironside
says, for example, that Moses represents those who, having
died, will be raised in glorified bodies, and Elijah depicts all
believers who, at the Rapture, will be caught up into heaven
without passing through death.[19] Be this as it may, the point we
wish to make about the Transfiguration is that it is a meeting
between the living—Jesus and His three disciples—and the
deceased, no matter how mysterious their dying.

There are those who believe this to be a visionary experience
and refer to the mention of appearing glory. R. T. France says
that the word *horama*, which is used by Jesus to describe the
event, largely refers to an inward experience like a trance or
vision.[20] The text does not support this use of the term here.
The Lucan parallel mentions how the two men are on the
point of leaving when Peter tries to delay their departure by
offering to build shelters. This is hardly the response of a man
undergoing a trance or a vision.

So what use can we make of this encounter between the dead
and the living? Again we accept that it is a sovereign moment
called by God for His own purposes. It is also worth pointing
out that Moses and Elijah appear in order to talk with Jesus
and not the disciples. Maclaren says that this event also teaches
us that Jesus is the Lord of all the living and the dead, and yet
care must be taken in drawing dogmatic conclusions from a
manifestly abnormal incident.[21] I do not think it is stretching the
evidence to say that the only meeting between the dead saints
and the living that are allowable are those sanctioned by God
and centered upon the Person of the Lord Jesus Christ.

THE HEALING OF LAZARUS

At first sight this story, told in John 11:1–44, might not strike us as a meeting between the living and the dead. Yet the fact of the matter is that Jesus speaks to a man who has been dead for at least four days. The dead man has had his funeral and been buried. Yet Jesus calls out loud, for all to hear, including the dead, "Lazarus, come out!" (John 11:43). The account continues, "The dead man came out, his hands and feet wrapped with strips of linen, and a cloth around his face" (verse 44). Perhaps this account more than any other speaks to us of the power of Jesus Christ to reach out to the dead and give them words of life. While we cannot use this passage to sanction any attempt to contact the dead, it does provide us with an encouragement that Jesus can speak to our dead and bring them His blessing.

It also helps us begin to understand that unresolved issues with the dead can be faced with Jesus. John Hampsch says that often after certain individuals have died, we may find that we are still carrying grudges against them. We may have to forgive them and, through Jesus, be forgiven on their behalf. He speaks of this as an unbinding of both the dead and the living, and uses the unbinding of Lazarus from his burial clothes as an illustration.[22]

Another interesting use of the Lazarus story is found in the book *Healing the Greatest Hurt* by Matthew and Dennis Linn and Sheila Fabricant. They suggest that this episode gives us a model for healing from the impact and consequences of a person's death upon the living.

They offer the following outline.

1. *Share your heart with Jesus (see John 11:1–41).*
   Here Mary and Martha pour out their hurt feelings to Jesus. Doubtless they are sharing how much they miss their brother and mingle their anger and frustration with their sorrow. It is also encouraging to know that Jesus does not refuse such emotion but shares it with them: Jesus weeps.

2. *Unbind and heal the deceased (see John 11:44).*

Just as Jesus speaks words of life to the dead, so, through Jesus, offer your own words of love and life to the deceased. This provides an opportunity to speak out any words that have been unsaid for however long. We have already noted how the dead in Christ continue to develop and grow after death; we can, therefore, offer prayers through Christ for their continued healing.

3. *Give thanks for new life (see John 11:42, 45).*
   Learn to include a spirit of celebration for the life of the dead. Such thanksgiving brings release to the living and joy to the dead.[23]

We can say that the living really do benefit from this kind of prayer because they are being enabled by the Lord Jesus to work through any unfinished material concerning the deceased. We cannot measure whatever benefits the deceased may receive, and we do not have any real scriptural evidence by which we can estimate what happens as a result of our prayers. Still the Lazarus story tells us that Jesus can speak healing to the dead, and so we can trust Him to speak such healing to our deceased as He wills in response to our prayers.

THE CLOUD OF WITNESSES

The cloud of witnesses mentioned in Hebrews 12:1, 22–24 is obviously those departed saints spoken of in the previous chapter who either conquered through faith or were called upon to give their lives in sacrifice for their faith. All alike, these ones who sought a better city than earth has as yet allowed have now died. The writer, in exhorting the Hebrew Christians to go forward in their faith, encourages the living by telling them that the deceased are watching their progress rather like spectators at the races in an amphitheater.

William Barclay says that this unseen cloud is a witness in a double sense, "for they have witnessed their confession to Christ and they are now witnesses of our performance. The

Christian is like a runner in some crowded stadium. As he presses on, the crowd looks down; and the crowd looking down are those who have already won the crown."[24] Some argue that because the Greek word for witness is *martureo*, it means strictly that the departed are not witnesses "of us" but witnesses "to us." With Maclaren, however, we are bound to say that such an idea of spectatorship is almost needed to give full force to the exhortation and imagery:

> It does seem a bit lame to say, you are like runners surrounded by a crowd of witnesses and therefore run, only do not suppose that they really see you. If this is so, the glowing imagery seems to receive a violent chill, and the flow of exhortation to be much choked.[25]

The obvious import of this passage is that we are not alone in our race of faith and life. God is with us through His Holy Spirit, but we have the saints in heaven to witness our running. We can only conclude that the point of their watching is to pray and urge us on. We have already glimpsed the fact that Revelation speaks of the saints interceding for the needs on the earth.

> Surely there is love in heaven, and maybe there is knowledge and it may be there is care for us. At all events the thought may come with cheer to our hearts that, whether conscious of one another's mode of being or not, they in their triumph and we in our toils are bound together with real bonds.[26]

I remember quite vividly watching television and learning that a Christian friend of mine, Wendy White, an Elim missionary in Zimbabwe, had been brutally killed along with all her fellow workers and their children. A week later I was sitting in a charismatic prayer meeting in Upton Hall Convent in Birkenhead when Sister Breda came in and said that, in her devotions, God had just reminded her that we were all being prayed for by Wendy who was now in heaven. I know it is only subjective, but I suddenly felt the rightness of what she said and felt comforted by Wendy. I felt I just had to thank God for His grace and His timely reminder that there is only one Body of Christ and when you die you do not suddenly leave it.

This idea of the corporate fellowship of all saints, living and departed, is also reinforced by the passage that speaks of the living coming to "thousands upon thousands of angels in joyful assembly. . . . You have come to God . . . to the spirits of righteous men made perfect . . . to Jesus" (Hebrews 12:22–24). Barclay treats this passage as dealing with the future benefits awaiting us in heaven. The setting, however, is in the present. And it speaks of Christians who, in worship of the living God, do not come alone before His throne. We come with the whole company of heaven.

It is from texts like this that the modern Anglican and Roman Catholic liturgies of Holy Communion speak of worshiping with the gathered company of the saints. The ancient creeds speak of "the communion of saints," and while referring obviously to the living they do not in any way exclude the deceased. As I read this passage I think we have, generally speaking, blundered grievously in severing heaven from earth. We think of these two spheres as being totally cut off from one another and having no communication. And the human heart has taken its revenge for such a divorce of the heavenly and the earthly. I am not for one minute condoning or advocating spiritism, but I think we need to see that one of the reasons for its popularity is the need for fellowship with those who have gone before, the desire to prove that heaven and earth are in communication with one another. "The only way in which we can combat spiritism is ourselves to rescue this truth about fellowship from the neglect into which it has fallen, to speak and think in a more Christian way about those who have passed on."[27]

So these two passages from Hebrews remind us that we belong to a fellowship of saints of all ages. While we may not be at liberty to speak to them, we are called upon to acknowledge and recognize them as fellow heirs of God's promises. They, in their turn, offer us support and encouragement. At the head and center of this ever-increasing family is Jesus, the Son of the Father.

THE SPIRITS IN PRISON

Before engaging in a discussion of 1 Peter 3:19 and 4:6, citing Jesus' preaching to the dead, we need to clarify just where it was that Jesus was preaching. The Apostles' Creed refers to this passage with the words *He descended into hell*. The correct word is *Hades*, and this term is the equivalent of the Old Testament word *Sheol*. Before Jesus' death and resurrection, Hades was the place where all the dead went awaiting judgment; hell is the place of punishment of the wicked. (These terms will be discussed further in the next chapter.)

Hades, like Sheol, was a shadowy world where the spirits of people moved like gray ghosts in an everlasting twilight. As time went on there emerged the idea of stages and divisions in this shadowland. The story of the rich man and Lazarus reflects this Jewish idea of a gulf separating the righteous and unrighteous dead. The unrighteous dead were thought to be kept in a kind of prison house in which they were held until the final judgment of God.[28]

It is to this shadowy world of the dead that Jesus comes; He gives homilies in Hades. There is some debate as to whether the spirits referred to are angels or the departed spirits of people. Some scholars suggest that the term *pneumata* ("spirits") is used only in this unqualified sense of supernatural beings and never of the departed.[29] Yet it is a fact that the term has been used of the human makeup in a variety of ways and seems naturally to refer to human beings at this juncture. This seems to be supported by the reference later on in Peter (see 1 Peter 4:6), which states specifically that Jesus preached the Gospel to those who were dead.[30]

Taking these two passages from 1 Peter together it seems that Jesus preached both specifically to those imprisoned for disobedience from the days of Noah and to the dead in general.

Barclay suggests that perhaps one of the reasons for preaching to the righteous dead would be to lead them out of Hades into the paradise of God.[31] In other words, Jesus was proclaiming His triumph fresh from Calvary, and this not only signaled the inevitable judgment of evil but the releasing of the captives who had been waiting for their full redemption. This is why the Christian promise is made that, from now on, those who die in the faith do not go to the shadowland of Hades but, being absent from the body, are present with the Lord in paradise. Perhaps this is also why Revelation 5:13 mentions that those "under the earth" also join in the song of redemption.

What is the purpose of Jesus preaching to the unrighteous dead? Is this, in fact, a second chance at salvation? Interestingly enough, Peter is very careful to include as part of this challenging passage the fact that Christ died once for all and that even the dead will have to face Jesus as their judge. This is, in fact, why the Gospel is preached in Hades, in order to make very clear the offer of salvation and the fact of judgment for those who reject this Gospel. It almost seems to be the parable of the rich man and Lazarus in reverse: No messenger from the dead comes to the living, but rather a messenger from the living comes down to the dead. Dr. Westcott in his book *Historic Faith* says that Christ in dying shared to the full our lot. His body was laid in the tomb. His soul passed into that state in which we conceive that our souls shall enter. He has won for God and hallowed every condition of human existence. We cannot be where He has not been. He bore our nature as living; He bore our nature as dead.[32]

We are not at liberty from this text to say that the unsaved are saved after they have died. I think we can say that the righteous are given a fuller glimpse of Him in whom they have put their hope. I think, too, we can accept that the result of such a revelation is that they enter into that same glory of God from which Elijah and Moses appeared on that day of transfiguration. This preaching in Hades is also to be seen as an act of love when the words of mercy and triumph are scattered in the pathway of those who have hoped, in the land of shadows, for a better day to dawn.

This speaking with the dead, therefore, is actually a completion of the work of the cross by which we who put our trust in Jesus as Savior have been saved and delivered from our sins.

Baptisms for the Dead

We come now to our final text that describes some form of meeting with the dead: 1 Corinthians 15:29. The most natural understanding of this verse is that some of the early believers got themselves baptized on behalf of friends who had died without receiving this sacrament. R. St. John Parry says that the plain and necessary sense of the words implies the existence of a practice of vicarious baptism at Corinth.[33] Parry goes on to say that for evangelicals the awkward thing is that, no matter how hard we try to dodge the issues of this passage, it is apparent that the apostle Paul refers to this practice without condemnation as proof for the reality of the resurrection. It must be pointed out, however, that Paul does not go on to commend the practice or mention it anywhere else in his writings. Barclay says that this custom sprang from a superstitious view of baptism, that, without it, a person was necessarily excluded from heaven.[34] This is not strictly true, however. This kind of belief actually gave rise to infant baptism, whereas the early practice was to delay baptism to the last possible moment on the grounds that as the sacrament washed away all sins then there would be little opportunity for forgiveness for further sins committed after baptism.

I do not think that the intention of such baptisms for the dead was that they might be saved and delivered into heaven as the Mormon Church practices. Such views had not been developed by that time. The most likely explanation is that it was an act of love for the dead by the living. Many different reasons are suggested, such as the dead were martyred before they were baptized, or that the Christian faith was still in its primitive stage and that the importance of the rite of baptism had not been appreciated by the deceased. The practice died out in the later Church presumably because persecutions eventually ceased and the sacrament became

more and more regularized in the life of the Church. Whatever
the real reason, the passage needs to be understood as an act of
commitment and love to the Christian dead. It is this point that
I wish us to take for ourselves in this book.

There is a tendency in the Western Church, once the eulogies
and the funeral services are over, to forget those who have died.
We need to cherish our dead and make acts of remembrance
and thank God for them at proper times and seasons. Where
appropriate, we need to love our saints and proclaim to them
also the great truths of the Gospel in the name of Jesus, who has
led the way. As an evangelical serving in a parish that regularly
reads out the names of the departed on the anniversary of their
deaths, I must testify that I came to appreciate the real sense
in which they were entering into the reality of the communion
of the saints.

In this chapter we have reviewed briefly the biblical insights
into relationships between the living and the dead. We see that,
while there is a definite ban on all forms of spiritualism, there
is indeed in the Person of Jesus Christ a crossing of the bound-
ary that separates these two parties. He speaks to the dead in
their world and allows them access to ours according to His
will and purpose. There is a place of meeting for the living and
the dead in the Body of Christ and in the context of worship
of the living God. There is also mention of acts of love and
commitment to the dead. There may be times when we have
to unbind our relationships with our dead, as the experience
of Lazarus illustrates. We have seen that there is also the oc-
casional gap in this division when the dead stray among the
living, as with the example of the dead Samuel.

We now have a basis for examining the way a Christian can
respond to people who say that they are troubled in some way
by those who have died. Before we can do this, however, we
need to understand how the Church developed these ideas.

3

Prayers, Purgatory and Protestants

To understand the way Christian thought about the dead developed in the first century and beyond, we need first to look at what was going on in Jewish theology at the time of Jesus. In all this, I think it is helpful to try to put ourselves in the shoes of the early Christians who were seeking after truth, being open to the Spirit, learning from the teaching and ministry of Jesus, working from the foundations of their Jewish heritage, yet all the while looking at life and death in the light of the momentous event of the death and resurrection of the Messiah. As they moved out into the Greek world to evangelize, so they also faced the added complications of Greek thought about death. But note that they had not been through the rigors of the Reformation. There was no Catholic/Protestant divide in their theology of the dead, so they had the advantage of not being burdened by prejudice.

Believers living in Old Testament times had hope of life after death (see Isaiah 26:19), but it was a vague hope. In

57

contrast they held a strong sense of power about the dead. Numbers 19:11–22 gives specific instructions to the people of Israel about dealing with a dead body, pointing out that it was absolutely vital to take every precaution. There was, of course, hygienic good sense in this. But remember that the ancient Hebrew was not separatist in his thinking about man as body, soul and spirit, and so he was aware that the dead body still had "spiritual power." It was reckoned that the soul of the deceased remained near the body for three days after death and, indeed, had some connection to it until total corruption had taken place. Thus, the body was greatly respected and the burial place most important.

Jewish Theology

BETWEEN THE TESTAMENTS

The inter-testamental period was a crucial time for the development of thought about the dead. This was a time of considerable turbulence for the Jews. The apocryphal book of Maccabees describes the exploits of some great heroes of faith, one outstanding leader being Judas Maccabaeus. In 2 Maccabees 12 we read the story of Judas defeating Gorgias, the governor of Idumea. Some Jews were killed in this battle and they needed to be buried. The story continues from verse 38 as follows:

> After the battle Judas led his men to the town of Adullam. It was the day before the Sabbath, so they purified themselves according to Jewish custom and then observed the holy day. By the following day it was urgent that they gather up the bodies of the men who had been killed in battle and bury them in their family tombs. But on each of the dead, hidden under their clothes, they found small images of the gods worshipped in Jamnia, which the Law forbids Jews to wear. Everyone then knew why these men had been killed. So they praised the ways of the Lord, the just judge, who reveals what is hidden, and they begged him that this sin might be completely blotted out. Then, Judas, that great man, urged the people to keep away from sin,

because they had seen for themselves what had happened to those men who had sinned. He also took up a collection from all his men, totalling about two kilograms of silver, and sent it to Jerusalem to provide for a sin-offering. Judas did this noble thing because he believed in the resurrection of the dead. If he had not believed that the dead would be raised, it would have been foolish and useless to pray for them. In his firm and devout conviction that all God's faithful people would receive a wonderful reward, Judas made provision for a sin offering to set free from their sin those who had died.

Judas Maccabeus.   GNB

It is perhaps helpful to notice various things about this passage:

1. The custom was to bury the dead in a family tomb. It was considered important to keep the family together, even in death.
2. Their idolatry was seen to be the cause of the death of these men, and they needed to be cleansed from it.
3. Judas believed in the resurrection of the dead and had a stronger view about the afterlife than the Old Testament view.
4. Because he believed in the hope of an afterlife, he deemed it necessary to pray for the men who had died in sin, believing that his prayer and the effect of the sacrifice would bring them freedom and their just reward.

Judas, living in the second century B.C., was one of those to whom God was revealing the idea of the resurrection of the dead. It was all part of the work of the Spirit, preparing people for the cross and resurrection of Jesus.

We need to recognize that this sort of story, about the great heroes of the faith, was very popular among the Jews of Jesus' day, and it was normal to pray for the dead. The problem for some of the Jews, particularly the Sadducees, was that they could not agree which books, apart from the Torah, could be considered as holy Scripture.

By the time of Jesus, those books known as the "Prophets" had won acceptance, but those called the "Writings" (which included the books of Maccabees) had not been unanimously accepted as canonical. Jesus quoted from these books freely (including some of the apocryphal books), and during the first three centuries the Apocrypha was generally used in the Church. But in the fourth and fifth centuries several of the early fathers started to doubt their authority and preferred the Scriptures that had been written in Hebrew. Though Ambrose, Augustine and other prominent leaders defended these books, Jerome did not favor them and his influence was considerable. The apocryphal books were rejected decidedly by the Protestants at the Reformation, whereas the Roman Catholics upheld their acceptance at the Council of Trent in 1546. The Jews incidentally continue to pray for the dead, and in their prayer book there can be found such prayers as:

> May God remember the soul of my revered father (mother) who has gone up to his (her) repose. May his (her) soul be bound up in the bond of life. May his (her) rest be glorious with fullness of joy in thy presence, and bliss for evermore at thy right hand.
>
> A prayer for the parent
> on the anniversary of his or her death[1]

JESUS AND THE DEAD

It is clear then that at the start of the first century A.D. we have a Jewish community that, apart from the Sadducees, was very much alive to the hope of the afterlife. First-century priest and historian Josephus wrote a discourse to the Greeks outlining his convictions about the afterlife. As a Pharisee he believed in an afterlife, and he supported the view that the soul, following death, goes to Hades, a place where souls are detained:

"There is one descent into this region, at whose gate we believe there stands an archangel with an host. . . . The just are guided to the right hand . . . the place we call the Bosom of Abraham." The just, therefore, went to the bosom of Abraham, but as to the unjust, "they are dragged by force to the left hand, by the angels allotted for punishment. . . . These angels . . . drag them into the neighbourhood of hell itself."[2]

Apart from the Sadducees, the Jewish people were at home with the concept of the afterlife. Prayers for the dead formed a regular part of synagogue prayers, which raises the interesting question of what Jesus and the early disciples did when they were in the synagogue. Did Jesus join in the synagogue prayers for the dead, or did He shut His lips at that point? We cannot base any teaching on this as it would be an argument from silence, but we do know that there is no recorded statement of Jesus opposing the custom. In His discussion with the Sadducees about resurrection (see Matthew 22:23–33), He says to them, "You know neither the Scriptures nor the power of God." God is powerful enough to make us like the angels after we die, and the Scriptures make it plain that the dead continue an existence after death. As was noted earlier, Jesus argues from Exodus 3:6 that the God who revealed Himself to Moses calls Himself "the God of Abraham, the God of Isaac and the God of Jacob," implying that Abraham, Isaac and Jacob are still very much "alive." The dead, far from being in some forgotten place, still have a reference to this life, not just as memories but as "the living."

The dramatic events of the first Easter and the Ascension gave a solid foundation for the Christian doctrine of salvation and the afterlife. This was not, however, a new doctrine replacing the old; rather, it was a natural development of the old. Jesus had gone to heaven as the firstfruits, and believers who put their faith in Jesus as the Messiah could now have assurance of sins forgiven. They were made just by the blood of the Lamb and their destiny by grace was heaven.

For the early Church, any questions about the status of the dead were irrelevant because they expected Jesus to return any day. As the years passed, however, it became evident that there might be a lapse of time before His return, and so it was natural for the Jewish practice of prayers for the dead to be accommodated into the Christian faith.

PRAYERS AND CULTS

As we consider how the early Christians developed their beliefs about the departed, we must always hold in mind that for them the separation between this world and the next was not as sharp as we might consider it. One of the places that marked the coming together of heaven and earth was the burial place of the deceased. Graves were not simply places where the body of the deceased lay "a-mouldering"; they were locations where in some mysterious way the soul was "present." It seems clear that in early Church history it was common practice to gather at the tomb of the one who had died in the faith of Christ. This was in part a way to respect and remember the death and work through grief. It was also a way to draw closer to the deceased to ask them for their prayers and also to ask God to bless them in paradise.

Early tomb inscriptions give us some clue as to what happened at early funeral services. Take a look at the following:

O Father of all, take into your keeping, Irene, Zoe and Marcellus whom you created. To you be the glory in Christ. (From the catacomb of Priscilla dated between A.D. 75 and 200.)

To our dearest Cyriacus, our sweetest son. May you live in the Holy Spirit. (From the catacomb of Callixtus, A.D. 200 to 300.)

Blessed Sozon gave back his soul aged 9 years. May the true Christ receive your spirit in peace, and pray for us. (From the catacomb of Gordian and Epimachus, A.D. 75 to 200.)

Pray for your parents Matronata Matrona, [you] who lived
one year and 52 days. (From the catacomb of the Lateran,
A.D. 200 to 300).[3]

I find these inscriptions very moving. They were not phrases
chosen from the stonemason's handbook. A great deal of
thought and feeling went into composing them, and they reveal
the depth of feeling that the bereaved had for their loved ones
who were dead but by no means forgotten. These inscriptions
are really quite enlightening. They indicate that the following
practices were normal in the early Church:

1. An act of commendation to God of the soul at death
   was normal.
2. They assumed that the departed existed "in the Holy
   Spirit." Life in the Spirit was an experience of this world
   and the next.
3. Prayer was made for the departed, asking fairly general
   things such as requesting that the departed would enjoy
   peace and be received by Christ.
4. It was assumed that one of the things that the departed
   would be doing in paradise was to pray for the living.

If you or I, then, had been a believer in those days and we
had lost a member of our family or a dear friend, we would
have taken the body to an appropriate burial place, thanked
God for him and prayed for him. We would respect the burial
place and return there, especially at anniversaries of birth and
death, and continue to ask God to bless him and to ask him
to pray for us. There is no doctrine here of salvation being
achieved through the intercession of the living for the dead.
Early Christians believed that salvation was achieved solely by
Jesus on the cross and not by their prayers.
As time went on, special regard was given to the burial
places of the martyrs. There is no doubt that reverence and
even mystique developed about these locations. The burial
places of the particularly pious became pilgrimage destina-

tions; churches were built over them (St. Peter's in Rome, for instance); the remains of their bodies became objects of devotion; and it became desirous to be buried as close as possible to a martyr, as this was reckoned to be of special benefit at the general resurrection. In many places this behavior got badly out of hand and the cult of the saints became a problem that church leaders had to face. There were terrible excesses, and one cannot help feeling that the lovely simplicity of the early years soon got lost in superstition and paganism.

What is interesting for our explorations, however, is the fact that the burial places of Christians of distinction were often places of spiritual power. It was not uncommon to hear testimonies of miracles, healing and deliverance taking place at the tombs of the saints. Thus, Jerome, writing in the early part of the fifth century, records an astonishing episode that a pilgrim called Paula experienced when she visited the tombs of some prophets in the Holy Land:

> She shuddered at the sight of so many marvellous happenings. For there she was met by the noise of demons roaring in various torments, and, before the tombs of the saints, she saw men howling like wolves, barking like dogs, roaring like lions, hissing like snakes, bellowing like bulls; some twisted their heads to touch the earth by arching their bodies backwards; women hung upside down in midair, yet their skirts did not fall down over their heads.[4]

When I first came across this passage I read it with considerable interest. I had been talking just the day before with someone who had had a great deal of experience in deliverance ministry, and he had related to me a number of stories where the same phenomena occurred. (I have to admit that he did not include incidents of women hanging upside down!) Jerome would have believed these tombs to be so spiritually charged that any demons coming near would have to flee. Hence, the deliverance phenomena. @ tombs of saints ?)

The inscription on the tomb of Martin of Tours reads:

Here lies Martin the bishop, of holy memory, whose soul is in the hand of God; but he is fully here, present and made plain in miracles of every kind.[5]

Such tombs were scenes of high activity and there was great expectation and faith for the miraculous. No doubt much of it was unhelpful and distracting; I am much happier about the Church on earth being responsible for the healing ministry. But we must recognize that there was something powerful at these places. Was it demonic power or the power of God? How on earth are we to understand these things?

Perhaps a way to view it is this. Imagine a man who in this world shows himself to be a man filled with the Spirit. He exercises charismatic gifts including healing and deliverance, and he is noted for being particularly pious and living close to God. During his ministry here on earth, he has a powerful ministry of intercession. Through living close to his Father in heaven, he is able to see where God is at work, and he has the faith to move mountains. Once he has died, he moves to paradise, and here he is much closer to God. He is free of the effects of the Fall, and he has entered the days of perfection.

The argument would run like this: If in his days of imperfection he was able to be such a channel of blessing, then in his days of perfection, from paradise, his ministry of intercession would be even more effective and powerful. Because his burial place is like a sign on earth of his existence, the natural place to come to him would be the grave. The grave becomes a sacrament—the outward visible sign of inward grace, which, in this instance, is the man who has died in faith and who now, unseen, is interceding for us. This assumes that you have some room for a belief that those in the world to come have some reference to those in this world. That is, we hold a belief that the saints pray for us.

I wonder if we in the 21st century have something to learn from our Christian ancestors? I find myself very cautious about this, because the whole area of spiritual power is fraught with danger. It seems to me that few in the early Church could handle this without moving fairly quickly into superstition or some sort of worship of the saints. Even for Jesus, it was a temptation to use spiritual power for His own ends by throwing Himself off the pinnacle of the Temple. It is a warning to us in these days, when we have such a wonderful release of God's power among us, that the Church down the centuries has often proved unable to handle it and has moved into idolatry.

In the matter of our subject, the power that—for whatever reason—was evident at the tombs soon became an object of fascination. And the dead—viewed no longer as servants of the grace of God and intercessors—were soon elevated to the status of gods, and cults developed. I feel sad as I view this piece of Church history. One cannot help feeling that these early Christians had discovered an important resource, but through misuse they lost it and promoted heresy.

PURGATORY AND HERESY

As years went by a doctrine came into being that gave a whole new purpose to praying for the dead. This was the doctrine of purgatory. *The Oxford Dictionary of the Christian Church* gives the following definition for purgatory:

> According to [Roman Catholic] teaching, the place or state of temporal punishment, where those who have died in the grace of God expiate their unforgiven venial sins and undergo such punishment as is still due to forgiven sins, before being admitted to the beatific Vision.

The Scriptures that have been used to support this doctrine are the passage from 2 Maccabees, already referred to, and two New Testament passages that we will now review.

Matthew 12:31–32. These are the well-known verses to do with blasphemy against the Holy Spirit. This in itself has puzzled Bible commentators down the ages, but what is also puzzling is Jesus' comment that this particular sin cannot be forgiven, "either in this age or in the age to come." I personally do not think you can build a doctrine on this because Jesus might simply be saying that sins will not be forgiven in the age to come, whatever happens. Many, however, have interpreted this verse as implying a possibility for post-death forgiveness.

First Corinthians 3:11–15. In this passage, Paul teaches that on the Day of the Lord our works will be revealed, by fire, to be made of either gold, silver, costly stones, wood, hay or straw. If it is one of the last three it will be burned up and the burning will be painful. The person will still be saved, however, "but only as one escaping through the flames." This is all in the context of teaching about divisions in the Church and God wanting to build temples, founded on Christ, as worthy habitations for the Spirit of God.

Clearly in the Corinthian church there was a fair bit of wood, hay and straw around, and Paul needed to be direct about it. But what exactly is this burning-up process that takes place when "the Day [brings] it to light"? Those who hold a view of purgatory say that this passage argues a case for purgatorial fire, a refining process, whereby all unconfessed and undealt-with sin is cleared away in preparation for the face-to-face meeting with Christ.

As we shall see in a moment, this view was summarily dismissed by the Reformers and by classical Protestantism. But before we shout Amen, should we not pause and ask the question, Is there truth here that got lost in heresy and anti-heresy hysteria? We need to remember that purgatory has always been viewed as a process that believers have to go through on their way to heaven; it is not designed for those destined for hell. So it should not be seen as a means by which people earn their way into heaven. Purgatory is regarded as being necessary for the saved, not the unsaved.

We find a development of the idea of purgatory in the early Church. Clement of Alexandria (died c. A.D. 215) taught that those who repent on their deathbeds but have no time to do penance in this life will be sanctified by the purifying fire in the next.[6] Ambrose (died A.D. 397) taught that those who die await the end of time in different places according to their immediate fate, which is decided by their works. Ambrose seems to be suggesting that there are waiting rooms of preparation before we enter heaven, and the waiting rooms represent different levels of purification. It was generally felt that martyrs had immediate passage to heaven and did not have to go through purgatory. Augustine (died A.D. 430) taught the absolute certainty of purifying pain in the next world in preparation for heaven.[7]

Thomas Aquinas amplified the teaching on purgatory. He taught that the guilt of venial sin is expiated immediately after death by an act of perfect charity, but that the punishment still has to be borne. He believed that the tiniest pain in purgatory is greater than the most severe pain on earth, but people can bear it because of the assurance of salvation, which gives the soul a deep peace. He taught that the prayers of the faithful on earth help the souls of the faithful departed through the painful journey of purgatory. The official teaching of the Roman Catholic Church on purgatory was defined at the Councils of Lyons (1274) and Florence (1439).

Again I need to point out that purgatory was a process deemed appropriate for Christians, not unbelievers. Prayer for those in purgatory was for hastening their passage through, not asking for their salvation. There was also a less clearly defined doctrine of "limbo," which was understood as a type of in-between state. Latin theology promoted one condition known as "the limbo of the fathers," meaning those who died at the time of the Old Covenant, and one known as "limbo of the children," meaning such people as infants who die unbaptized. According to Augustine's view, they are in a state of original sin but are innocent of personal guilt.

As we shall see in a moment, the doctrines of purgatory and limbo were greatly abused in the Middle Ages and got well and truly thrown out by the Reformers. But, again, it is perhaps interesting to note that, had we been members of the early Church, we would have held to a view of purgatory. Is there any truth in this that we need to pick up today?

It seems to me that there is room in the gospels for a belief in some sort of intermediate process between the moment of death and that moment when we shall see our Lord Jesus, face to face on that glorious day. Dr. Kenneth McAll calls this place not purgatory but a convalescent home. His understanding is that we need a place where we can recover from the wounds of sin and come gradually into the light. Brother Ramon prefers to use the word *sanctificatory*. Ramon describes this process thus:

> I do not mean that there would be no suffering—but that it would not be penal, a suffering of retribution or payment, but rather the kind of suffering that the believer knows in this life as the Holy Spirit sears and burns him in the crucible of the divine Love.[8]

Ramon goes on to do a type of exposition of Newman's "Dream of Gerontius," which describes the journey through death. When Gerontius dies, he is met by the angel who has guided him all through his life. This angel then leads him through the process that enables the interior transformation to take place where he can see face to face the "Holiest in the height." Ramon is someone who is held in respect by a wide cross section of Protestants. I think it is the case that breaking down the iron curtain between Protestant and Catholic means that we can look at this doctrine of purgatory in an open way, rather than concentrating on guarding the walls.

What, then, can we believe about purgatory? First, let me say that, in my view, we need to drop the word *purgatory* as it has too many unhelpful connotations. I like Dr. McAll's idea of the convalescent home, and one might be right in saying that this place is actually paradise. I have been greatly helped in my understanding of life after death by Jim Graham's *Dying to Live*.[9] His understanding of Scripture leads him to conclude that a type of two-stage process takes place after death:

1. At death, we leave our bodies and become discarnate spirits. Those who are saved, like the thief on the cross, go immediately to paradise. *Paradise* is a Persian word and means an exquisite garden. This new Garden of Eden is the place of waiting, a place of great beauty, a type of foretaste of things to come. For the unsaved, their destination is Hades, the prison referred to in 1 Peter 3:19. Again, paradise is a place for discarnate spirits. Gardens in the Bible are always places full of significance and imagery. There is the first garden, the Garden of Eden, a place of such promise, and yet the place of temptation and the scene of the fall of mankind. There is the Garden of Gethsemane, the place of agony, the place of Jesus accepting the will of the Father and setting His face to the cross. It is the place of prayer and the dark night of the soul. Then there is the Easter garden, the place of resurrection and transformation. It is the spring garden of hope, where the rivers of life flood over the drab wilderness of death. Paradise is the ultimate garden. In paradise is the beauty of Eden and the resurrection glory of the Easter garden. And maybe there is also a Gethsemane part to this garden, that refining process whereby all that is against the will of God in us is taken away, and we are made perfect by the blood of the Lamb. Paradise is the place where our bodies sleep, but our spirits remain active and very much alive.[10]

2. The second stage is where our bodies wake. This will be the general resurrection. Just as Jesus spent some time in paradise as a discarnate spirit and then went on to become reunited with His transformed earthly body, so we also will enjoy a resurrection body (see 1 Corinthians 15). To use Jim Graham's picture, this is moving from the garden into the house, the house of many mansions. This is heaven, the proper place for those who are redeemed. Here we exist for eternity enjoying the full presence of the Lord. This is the place of the new heaven and the new earth. At this time the unsaved move from the prison

of hades to hell. As I understand it, hell is the place of full separation from God. That means there can be no life, and that, therefore, means annihilation. This is the ultimate sadness for creatures that have been destined for eternity, but God is perfectly just, and choices that individuals have made here on earth will be honored in heaven.[11]

In all this, then, I am suggesting that at death those who are saved will enter paradise in a discarnate state. Paradise will include some sort of refining process, which is described in 1 Corinthians 3:11–15. This has nothing to do with our destiny; it has to do with preparation and holiness. It is the convalescent home, the "sanctificatory" where that which was begun when we first came to Christ will be completed. All this is in preparation for that most wonderful of days when, fully perfected and more alive than we have ever been in this world, we shall dwell with God in the new heaven and the new earth.

PROTESTANTS AND PREJUDICE

It is very hard for Protestants to think dispassionately about the subject of purgatory and prayer for the dead because this was one of the key subjects that brought about the Reformation. By the fourteenth century this doctrine had been dreadfully corrupted; the evil practices of selling indulgences had developed, and the poor and vulnerable were manipulated by threats about purgatory. Few of the faithful looked forward to heaven, as the prospect of a horrendous journey through purgatory filled their minds. Salvation and purgatory had gotten confused, and the simple Gospel truth of salvation by faith had long been lost. Indulgences and prayers for the dead were seen as means of winning God's favor and achieving salvation, and it is probably true that many never heard the message of the cross.

It is not surprising, then, that when the bright new light of the Reformers swept across Europe, fueled by the rediscovery of salvation by faith alone in the atoning work of the cross, this particular doctrine was one of the first to be attacked. Quite rightly the terrible abuses were dealt with and great freedom was brought to the faithful. Perhaps we cannot fully appreciate what a liberation this was. Few of the Reformers were in the frame of mind to explore these doctrines any more closely than they had to. There was to be no turning back, no giving of ground to anything other than the Gospel of salvation by faith.

Thus, prayers for the dead were dispersed from the life of the Protestant Church. Cranmer did include a prayer for the deceased in his 1549 rite, "At the Burial," which asked that the "sinnes whiche he committed in this world be not imputed unto him, but that he, escaping the gates of hell and the paynes of eternall darkness may euer dwell in the region of lighte." This prayer was removed by 1552. Generally prayers that focused on the dead were seen to undermine the work of the cross. People were saved in this life; there was no possibility of salvation after this life. Because they equated prayer for the dead with prayer for the salvation of the departed soul, they had no use for it.

In time, however, the doctrine started to gain currency. The Tractarians reintroduced the idea of purgatory and called it "the intermediate state." It is on this that Newman based his "Dream of Gerontius."

There was also one other occasion that led to a revival in prayer for the dead, and that was the severe and agonizing experience of bereavement faced by millions of families during the First World War. R. J. Campbell wrote in 1916 that he believed the war would bring back a more definite doctrine of the communion of saints. Protestantism had "little comfort to give to mourners, for it has been so sadly silent regarding the fate of our dead."[12] During the war some of the strongest evangelicals changed their views about prayers for the dead. Alan Wilkinson writes:

Bishop Moule of Durham, a staunch Evangelical, though he deplored medieval practices, said that he gave 'perpetual greetings' to the departed; it was certainly 'no sin' to follow them with '*suspira*' that they might enjoy ever-growing light and joy in heaven.[13]

In 1917 Archbishop Randall Davidson actually wrote and issued a prayer for the deceased, which was explicitly for deceased soldiers that they might be "accounted worthy of a place among the faithful servants in the Kingdom of heaven."[14] Of course this was coming straight out of the "valiant hearts" theology that those who gave their lives for their country were in a mysterious way identified with Christ who gave His life for the world. Many criticized this quasi-Islamic belief, but, nonetheless, the practice of praying for the departed was widespread and gave great comfort to many. It does support the view that those who are in grief have a legitimate need to find an appropriate way of continuing a relationship with a deceased loved one and to find Christian ways of expressing it.

When we talk about relationships with our Roman Catholic brothers and sisters, we find that sooner or later we come up against these doctrines. And it is often at this point that we discover that our beliefs are not based on truth but on prejudice. Talk to many of an evangelical persuasion and they will dismiss any notion of praying for the dead and not take kindly to discussion on purgatory. But I have to wonder how much serious thinking they have done on the subject. Have they listened to the Catholic point of view? Is their belief based on genuine searching for the truth, or on prejudices that have been uncritically absorbed into their subconscious?

It is my belief that there is ground between Catholic and Protestant views about the dead that we can move to. But it will mean dealing with some of our prejudices—and some roots of bitterness that started four hundred and fifty years ago with the Reformation still require healing.

So where has all this gotten us? We have traveled speedily through history; are we any the wiser? I am conscious that I have raised more questions than I have answered, and on these sorts of issues I find the fence a peculiarly attractive place upon which to sit. Having explored the territory, however, I think we have made a few discoveries:

1. It soon becomes evident that, in approaching a subject like this, it is essential to exercise humility. We are all going to have lots of surprises when we die and find out what the other side is really like. It would be foolish to try and claim too much. We need to be humble in our attitude to others. The doctrines discussed above are held dear by many of our Christian neighbors, and they are worthy of respect. We need to listen and to learn. And there will be times when we have to let go of things that we have cherished uncritically over many years. We must invite the Spirit of all truth to lead us.

2. It seems to me that it does not run counter to biblical truth to admit to some sort of purifying process in paradise. I do not think we can claim much more than that. But if this is the case, it should encourage us all the more to see that the process of healing, wholeness and holiness is going on in that world. I actually take a lot of comfort from the thought that after death there will be a time of preparation before I meet Jesus. To use rather a trite analogy, I would rather go to my wedding having had a good shower and changed into the proper clothes, than turn up dirty and in my working clothes, even though I know I am loved and accepted whatever I am wearing. Maybe the changing process will take a split second, maybe it will take longer—who knows, and what does time mean anyway in paradise!

3. Early tradition supports the practice of prayers for the dead. These prayers were not meant to affect the salvation of the deceased. Rather, they were acknowledging that the deceased were still part of the community of faith, but that they had left earth and were in paradise. There seems to be nothing wrong with offering prayers

to God for the deceased, which essentially express our love for them and our hope that they are enjoying peace in Christ. Pastorally, this may be a most helpful practice for those who are suffering bereavement. It needs to be treated with some caution as I foresee two dangers.

First, some people need to be helped into a proper letting go of the deceased, and so this kind of prayer may hinder them. (Some people, however, find it hard to let go precisely because there is no obvious way of remembering the deceased. To pray in the way I have described may actually help the letting-go process. So discernment will be needed.) Second, for those who are not committed Christians, encouragement to pray for the dead may raise hopes that salvation can be procured after death. Folk religion thrives on such hopes. We need to see that this is a discipline for the faithful.

4. Prayers *by* the dead is something that most Christians probably believe in. Most understand the "cloud of witnesses" in Hebrews 12:1 as being the company of the faithful who are, so to speak, in the grandstand cheering us on. This is a tremendous resource. For all its faults, the early Church was probably on to something when it recognized the spiritual power in the prayers of the saints. The difficulty comes in knowing how to avail ourselves of this prayer backing. Do we need to ask, or is it there automatically? Do we ask the saints directly, or do we ask Jesus? Never underestimate the very real problems associated with direct requests to saints. Such a practice moves us away quickly from concentration on Jesus. At its worst we make gods of the saints. My feeling is that we should recognize the strength of this backing and, just as we might ask God to send His angels to defend and help us, so we might appropriately ask Him to urge the saints to pray for us. This is not just a theological nicety. We are living in days when the spiritual battle is intense, and I believe it is in this realm of the spiritual battle that the prayer backing of the saints can be so helpful. Imagine

people like the Wesleys, C. T. Studd, Arthur Wallis, Dorothy Kerin, David Watson and others, all people of great faith when they were here on earth, who now no longer see through a glass darkly, but who see perfectly and can pray perfectly for us. They can see the principalities and powers in ways that we cannot. We know what prayer warriors they were when they were on earth; just think what they are like now! I am not being flippant here—I am pointing out that there is a tremendous resource of strength available for when we are engaged in the battle. This should encourage us.

5. The company of heaven knows how to worship the Lord. There are many references in the book of Revelation to the faithful worshiping God. I love the part of the Anglican Communion service where we remind ourselves that we are in the company of "angels and archangels and all the company of heaven," and together, in some way mystically joined in our act of worship, we utter together, "Holy, Holy, Holy Lord, God of power and might. . . ." It lifts my spirit when I come into worship to think I am joining that great worship going on in paradise.

6. Any talk of paradise or heaven must inevitably excite the hope within us. In the West our vision of the afterlife is often very feeble. The early Church was fired by a clear, wonderful, unassailable vision of heaven. We need to dwell on the things of heaven—not as escapism but rather to deepen our involvement in this world. We are the citizens of heaven who bring the Good News of another Kingdom to a world that has lost the vision. The disciple is one who is called to be a visionary, to carry in his or her heart the highway to Zion. Those who have such a highway in their hearts are the ones who are able to walk through even the valley of tears and turn them into springs of life. Those who have some understanding of the things of heaven "go from strength to strength, till each appears before God in Zion" (Psalm 84:7).

4
Hurtings and Hauntings

It was a warm summer night and I awoke in the small hours. I was living at this time in an old house in Buckinghamshire, part of which dated back to the thirteenth century. I was alone in the room, but I awoke because I sensed I had company. Instinctively I felt afraid because I had that curious sense that something supernatural was happening. I looked across to the far window, and there, as calmly as the summer night itself, stood a man reading by the light of the moon. He wore a cloak, and his stooped head supported a wide-brimmed hat. I felt terrified! Within moments the man had gone and I was alone in my room again, praying fervently and longing for the dawn!

Now the question is, What exactly did I see? At that time I was about twenty years old and a keen member of my university Christian Union. In those days things were either black or white. What I had seen had frightened me, and the evangelical/Pentecostal teaching that I had received on this sort of thing was that ghosts were evil and were a demonic impersonation. So, academically, if you like, I was satisfied that I had been subject to a spiritual attack. This is one perfectly plausible explanation, and one I stood by for some time. But I was not entirely satisfied and I found myself daring to probe a little deeper into this phenomenon, all the while anxious that I should not slide down the slippery slope into spiritualism.

Thus an ongoing debate ran in my mind like this:

"The man was a messenger of Satan, a demon disguised, and the purpose was to terrify you."

"Well, that may be true, but, on the other hand, I cannot deny that this man had no evil intention that I could make out. In fact he seemed quite gentle and did not really seem to notice me."

"That's just how spiritualists talk! They make out that all this stuff about the dead is really very safe and attractive. Go further down this track and you will soon find yourself approaching mediums and trying seances to contact the man."

"I loathe the thought of going off to seances in an attempt to contact this man or any dead person for that matter. I am simply trying to suggest that this 'thing' may not have been a demon at all but may have been a departed human spirit, who, for some reason best known to himself, turned up in my bedroom on that particular night."

And so the argument would go.

An interesting little detail did emerge some time after this incident. I discovered that the house where we lived had been a popular meeting place for Quakers, and even George Fox himself stayed there. When I looked up drawings of Quakers they were dressed similarly to my gentleman. And so, I ask, Was this the spirit of one of the early Quakers?

Now I relate this incident because it is my impression that many people have their own personal stories to tell about ghosts. I believe that a lot of Christians are afraid to talk about these experiences for fear that they will receive condemnation in return. Many Christians actually do face rejection for having experienced a supernatural or psychic event of this sort. They may be suspected of having spiritist tendencies, or being demon-possessed, or simply being rather odd and not quite the sort of person one should be having fellowship with.

Because the experience is common, we need to work hard at understanding it, and we have to learn how to pastor those who need to relate such experiences in a safe environment.

What Is a Ghost?

So what exactly is a ghost? How can we make sense of such phenomena? Using the above story as an example, here are five popular explanations:

1. Psychological

Some would say that my experience was a type of vivid hallucination. They might explain that it was like an extension of a deeply felt dream and, with the help of shadows playing tricks, a rich dinner and a lively late-adolescent mind, I believed I saw something that in reality was not there. There is no doubt that in some circumstances, such as severe grief, the internal power of longing can be so strong that it becomes hard to distinguish fact from fantasy.

Parapsychologists refer to a phenomenon known as "crisis apparition." This describes that experience when one person in one particular place "sees" someone he knows who is in another place, and who is in some kind of trauma, or may be dying, or may have recently died without the other person being aware of it. I remember a close friend describing this kind of experience. Her husband was traveling away from home on business. In the night she was awakened by a terrible dream in which she saw her husband reaching out to her, appealing to her for help. Moments later she got a phone call telling her that her husband had died from a heart attack in the night while staying in a motel. She never knew how to understand this experience and felt distinctly uncomfortable about telling this story in Christian company.

In 1987 the Christian Exorcism Study Group produced a report called *Deliverance*, subtitled "Psychic Disturbances and Occult Involvement." It states:

The generally accepted explanation among para-psychologists is that such crisis apparitions do not involve the perception of a quasi-material 'ghost' or 'astral body' of the second person, but result from the first person receiving some sort of [telepathic?] message which is then exteriorized in apparitional form, sometimes at the very moment of crisis, but sometimes delayed by a number of hours or even days.[1]

We are presented, then, with the possibility that the mind has considerable power to imagine another in such a way as to actually experience with one or more of the senses the presence of the other who may be dead or in a different place. There is also the possibility of a communication between minds that is commonly called *telepathy*.

It is worth noting again that there will be in most churches Christian folk who have had some psychic or paranormal experience about which they feel uneasy and yet find hard to share. The difficulty in sharing comes from the feeling that others within the Christian community will make judgments about them, which can be hurtful. They may well be laughed at, ostracized or considered to be involved in witchcraft. This can make people very wary of sharing their experiences.

I can recall several occasions when people have come to me, owning up to such experiences and confessing them as a deep burden. The burden is increased by all the teaching (albeit necessary) about the horrors of the occult. I remember one person who for many years had premonitions of disasters; this was a psychic gift she could well have done without. It came to a head for her when she had a premonition of the sinking of the *Herald of Free Enterprise* and she came to me for help. Together in prayer we offered this unwanted psychic ability to God, and I prayed for her to be cleansed from it. The result was that she became free of it and also felt a new freedom in her Christian life. She was one who found freedom, but my guess is that there are many more who do not because they are fearful of sharing such things in Christian fellowship. We need to allow people to share their stories without threat of condemnation, so that they can experience the freedom of Jesus.

Under this heading, then, we are acknowledging that many curious things go on in the mind, which is subject to hallucination and psychic disturbances of one sort or another. It is possible, therefore, that ghost phenomena, such as my Quaker gentleman, are a product of the complexity of the mind and may indicate a weakness or area of unwholeness that needs cleansing and healing.

2. Place Memory

This explanation of ghosts works on the assumption that some places are charged with memories from the past that can be picked up and projected out onto the present. There is no clear way of understanding or explaining this, but it does seem to be the case that certain places do attract ghost activity where the particular ghost, when sighted or heard, is doing the same thing over and over again.

It can be compared with the experience of listening to music on the radio and picking up, quite unexpectedly, a message from a police patrol car. You think you are tuned into your favorite radio station but suddenly find that you are listening for a few seconds to something totally different. In the same way, we are "tuned" to pick up the wavelength of the here and now, but just occasionally some people have an ability to pick up something from the past. They just happen to be receivers of this type of "memory," and they project it in such a way that they, and sometimes other observers, may witness a scene from the past. They observe something like a clip of a video—that is, not the real thing, but an impression of it.

To go back to my Quaker, the understanding according to this definition would be that I was experiencing a "memory," a sort of photograph of this gentleman, and something about me at that particular time triggered this "memory" into being.

I have found no adequate way of testing this theory scientifically, but I can see some sense in it.

3. Impersonation

I mentioned that in my late teens and early twenties I had what I thought was a clear-cut understanding of ghosts. The book that influenced me more than any other was *The Challenging Counterfeit* by Raphael Gasson. This book was written by a man who once was deeply involved in spiritualism as a medium and had considerable knowledge of and experience with spiritualist and psychic phenomena. Following his dramatic conversion to Christ, he renounced his old ways. His book is an attempt to present the Christian Gospel of truth and hope over against the deceptions of spiritualism. The book has undoubtedly helped many and has been a significant contribution to Christian anti-occult literature.

The conclusion he comes to in his understanding of ghosts is that they are demons impersonating the spirits of dead relatives and that their main purpose is to seduce people into the bondage of spiritualism. He argues very convincingly that Satan has a well-developed system of counterfeiting the spiritual gifts and is out to deceive all who stray near to this dangerous path. The spirits who communicate through mediums are, according to Gasson's understanding, clearly demonic:

> In view of the statements of Scripture which must remain the only measuring rod for all true Christians, there is only one conclusion that a Christian can arrive at, and that is that the spirits which so communicate, are not highly evolved 'spirit guides' and the souls of dead persons, but actually demons impersonating dead people. This may sound strange and unreal to those who have little or no contact with the principalities and powers of darkness, but to the student of Scripture, it is no new thing. . . . The demons, pretending to be the spirits of the departed, have to tread very carefully and they begin in a very plausible way and gradually ensnare those who are investigating out of mere curiosity.[2]

There is no doubt in my mind that spiritualism is an occult religion and completely contradicts all the glorious biblical truths about the promise of the afterlife. Nothing in either the Old or New Testaments suggests that believers may go round trying to make contact with the dead. Given, then, that spiritualism is occultic, does it necessarily follow that all ghost phenomena are demonic impersonation? Let's begin with the subject of contacts through mediums.

Scripture teaches about deceptive spirits and the need to discern the spirits. This suggests that in the spiritual realm nothing can be taken at face value; the powers of deceptiveness are strong. Demons in the New Testament generally manifest themselves as unseen destructive forces operating in individuals' lives rather than disguising themselves as ghosts. Nonetheless, given the existence of demons and given the deceptive nature of spiritualism, there is a strong likelihood that mediums do make contact with demonic influences that can impersonate the relatives of the dead.

The conclusion I have personally come to is this: Some mediums have occult powers enabling them to make contact with deceiving demons who disguise themselves as the dead relatives of those present or as the spirit of some significant person who has died and has something "important" to communicate to the living.

The ouija board is a popular medium through which people try to make contact with the dead. In my teenage years I remember being invited to be part of a group using an ouija board (to be precise I think it was an upturned glass on a table, which in some ways made it even more mysterious—did the spirit climb inside the glass, one wondered?). We were all rather alarmed when the spirit informed us that his name was "Winston." As Winston Churchill had died only a short while before this incident, we were quite convinced it was he, but we could think of no questions important or intelligent enough to ask of such a distinguished visitor, and my excursion into ouija was brought to an abrupt end!

I do want to add hastily that I have since renounced any connection with ouija and recognize the sinister powers at work in this medium. I also feel I need to say that, in this particular case, the glass was probably moved by us rather than an unseen force. But it is the sort of situation where some malignant spirit could ensnare unsuspecting schoolboys who thought they were communicating with a departed spirit. In fact, not long after this another group of pupils tried it with the glass and one of the boys was badly affected and had some sort of a fit as a result. He had clearly made contact with a demonic power.

It may also be that some mediums actually do make contact with departed spirits. If this is the case they will make contact with the "unquiet dead" (see next section) rather than those who are resting in peace. When this happens, the medium becomes guilty not so much of deception but of cruelty, because the proper contact with any such dead should be to send them away from this world, not to continue to hold them here.

Kenneth McAll, in his *Healing the Haunted*, tells the story of a family who moved into a large house in the south of England. The house had been the home of a well-known spiritualist writer who had since died. The house had a reputation for being haunted by this man, who apparently came back looking for his diary. When the family experienced various manifestations, which suggested that the dead writer was still around the house, the father visited the vicar who came and said prayers of release. The house became peaceful and there were no further manifestations. Interestingly, not long after this a short article appeared in a daily newspaper reporting that a medium had received a message from that spiritualist writer. McAll notes:

> A few days later, a short article appeared in the *Daily Mail* saying that Madame Roberts, a famous medium in Kent, had at last received a message from this writer. Before he died he had promised that he would come back but never had done so and no one had ever 'met him' or heard anything from him, in spite of many attempts to arrange meetings. Now he was

saying to the medium, 'I wish to apologise for having misled people during my life'.[3]

In this instance it seems that Madame Roberts was successful in contacting the deceased. Perhaps in this instance it was permitted by God so that she might be brought to truth.

The conclusion thus far, therefore, is that in the world of spiritualism, mediums often do make contact with deceptive spirits or demons that impersonate the dead. But this is not universally the case, as there appear to be some genuine examples of the dead being contacted. The dead who are contacted are reckoned to be among the unquiet dead.

I have written so far about contacts through mediums. There are, of course, many contacts with the dead that have nothing to do with mediums and spiritualism. Here I return to my test case of the Quaker. Was this ghost a demon impersonating a Quaker, as I believed at the time? Presumably if it had been demonic impersonation, the intention was either to frighten me or to lure me into the fascination about the dead and, therefore, into spiritism or some other stream of the occult.

The experience certainly frightened me, though I do wonder a bit why a demon would have to disguise himself as a Quaker in order to frighten me. Could he not simply appear as himself or play other nasty tricks? And although I was frightened, I was frightened not so much of the thing as of the fact that I was witnessing something supernatural. The testimony of some who saw angels in the Bible is that they were terrified (see Matthew 28:4, which describes how the guards on the tomb of Jesus who saw the angel were so terrified that they became like dead men). So the fact that I was frightened does not necessarily mean that the thing was evil. Regarding the possibility that this experience was intended to lure me into spiritualism, I can only say that I wasn't!

There is, of course, no foolproof test one can do to say whether or not this was demonic. The main guide comes from a gift of the Holy Spirit mentioned in l Corinthians 12:10: the ability to distinguish between different kinds of spirits. Un-

fortunately for us Western cerebral thinkers, this gift comes
from that subconscious area of instinct and intuition, which, of
course, makes it "unreliable." Or does it? The Bible never puts
a higher value on the more cerebral gifts. But there is no denying that when we come into the area of intuition it is harder to
talk about things like "proof" and "certainty." I would venture
to say, however, that according to my intuition, which I think
may house some God-given ability to distinguish spirits, my
impression is that this nighttime visitor who came to my home
was not a demon.

4. The "Unquiet Dead"

The report from the Christian study group, *Deliverance*,
contains a chapter on the unquiet dead and argues that ghost
phenomena may well be appearances of the spirits of the dead,
the souls of those departed from this life who are not at rest
and are therefore said to be "unquiet." The counselor who is
helping someone troubled by such a phenomenon

> is forced to consider as a possible hypothesis that some par-
> ticular and identifiable individual, though departed this world,
> is 'earthbound', and keeps troubling a person or place with
> which during his life he had particularly strong emotional ties.
> The ghost of someone may be seen in the place where he lived
> or worked or died, and his appearance may be observed by
> independent witnesses who sometimes do not know him or the
> circumstances of his life and death until they make inquiries and
> discover them. In many cases the person whose ghost is seen
> will have died suddenly, tragically, or unexpectedly.[4]

The report goes on to say that the spirit of a dead person may
manifest itself in this world for one of three possible reasons:

A. The spirit has been too strongly attached to a place or
   person before death and cannot let go; it resents the present occupier of its beloved place and resents the making
   of new relationships from which it is now excluded.

B. The spirit is distressed at being trapped in this world and is attracting attention as a cry for help.
C. The spirit may be giving comfort as best it can to a person whom it has loved dearly and who is missing its physical presence.

According to this definition, then, the apparition that I saw was actually the soul of a departed Quaker. For some reason this man, following his death, had become trapped in some sort of limbo world where it was possible for him, on occasions, to appear to the living. Maybe this particular window was one that he strongly loved. Maybe he died a tragic death. Maybe he was trying to call my attention to release him to the afterlife. It is this category that particularly interests Dr. McAll. Our next chapter deals with it more thoroughly.

This way of associating the dead with a type of limbo land is not easy for evangelicals to digest. It does not fit neatly into our established ways of thinking about death and the afterlife. But my feeling is that our efforts to make the thing neat and tidy have restricted our vision, and certainly when one is dealing with the afterlife it would be foolhardy to try to be too neat and tidy. Obviously a great deal here is mysterious and unknown and we have to speculate. The fact is that these psychic phenomena do exist, they do trouble people and sometimes disturb them deeply, and we do need to find ways of understanding them so that we can deal with them.

There is another side to this, too. If my Quaker really was a discarnate spirit, an unquiet dead, appealing to me for help, then this brings in a whole new area of responsibility for me. It means that I have responsibility toward not only the living but the dead.

As someone who is in holy orders this is nothing new to me. At every funeral service I take, I am responsible for commending the soul to God. In the case of the Quaker, had I entered into some sort of requiem, I would simply have been doing what I would normally do at a funeral service, only many years after the death.

5. Legitimate Appearances of the Dead

We have looked at how ghost phenomena may be discarnate spirits "stuck" in this world against their will who need some sort of help from us to release them. There is one last category: The discarnate spirit has been sent back to this world legitimately. That is, it seems that there may be occasions where God chooses to communicate something crucial to someone on earth, and He chooses one of the company of heaven to achieve it. In chapter 2 we looked at some biblical examples of this, notably the visit of Moses and Elijah with Jesus at the Transfiguration.

I have often been intrigued by the strange events going on in Jerusalem following the death of Jesus as recorded by Matthew. So momentous was the act of Jesus giving up His spirit that it had a dramatic effect on nearby matter (earth shook and rocks split) and the

> tombs broke open and the bodies of many holy people who had died were raised to life. They came out of the tombs, and after Jesus' resurrection they went into the holy city and appeared to many people.
>
> Matthew 27:52–53

What are we to make of that? I have yet to find a satisfactory explanation for these tantalizing verses. I would not want to draw too many conclusions, but I do note various things:

A. The incident happened in connection with the separation of Jesus' spirit from His earthly body, and also with the union of His spirit with His resurrected body.

B. Matthew particularly points out that the bodies of the people rose. We are dealing, therefore, with resurrected bodies, not ghosts.

C. He also mentions that we are dealing with holy people going into a holy city. The absence of sin is interesting. The point of this exercise seems to be that some selected holy people were called by God to declare the glorious truth of the victory of Jesus over death.

This does seem to suggest that there are cases of a legitimate visit by the departed to someone in this world. There are, of course, a number of testimonies to this effect. When I was a curate I remember having the privilege of visiting Iris, an elderly lady who was dying of leukemia. She had suffered terribly in her later years, but she was one of those people who had an inner light that suffering seemed to fuel rather than quench. As a rather naive young curate I would go to "minister" to her, and, of course, I always came away having been ministered to by her.

Not long before her death she was, she claimed, visited by her deceased mother who came to reassure her and tell her about the preparations being made for her arrival in heaven. When she talked of these visits, it was as if she had peeped into heaven itself. Those of us who have been with the dying have probably known a number of people who have had this experience.

And what are we to make of it? Is it psychological, something to do with the stress of dying? Is it a place-memory or a demon in disguise? Is it an unquiet spirit? Well, in the case of Iris none of these answers is satisfactory. The only answer I am satisfied with is the notion that at certain crisis times, like death, the departed are permitted to come as encouragers because, after all, they are part of that great cloud of witnesses who surround us.

Although this sort of experience is common at or near the time of death, there are other testimonies to this happening at other times. There is that curious story in *Ring of Truth*, for example, where J. B. Phillips has an experience of meeting the spirit of C. S. Lewis:

> Many of us who believe in what is technically known as the Communion of Saints, must have experienced the sense of nearness, for a fairly short time, of those whom we love soon after they have died. . . . The late C. S. Lewis, whom I did not know very well and had only seen in the flesh once, but with

whom I had corresponded a fair amount, gave me an unusual experience. A few days after his death, while I was watching television, he 'appeared' sitting in a chair within a few feet of me, and spoke a few words which were particularly relevant to the circumstances through which I was passing.[5]

In the Catholic tradition are numerous examples of Mary and other saints appearing and giving messages. In recent years a great deal of interest has grown in the messages apparently given by Mary to the children at Medjugorje in Yugoslavia. It is impossible to know how to judge these appearances, but there does seem to be sufficient evidence to suggest that God, under certain circumstances, does permit a soul to visit this world for the purpose of communicating an important message.

HEALING THE HURTS

Whether we like it or not, experiences of hauntings and encounters with the dead are fairly common, and those of us who are part of the Church of Jesus Christ, who is the glorious conqueror of death, are responsible for trying to understand them. We will need to seek God for discernment to enable us to distinguish the right cause of the particular phenomenon. If the cause is psychological, then the person who experienced it will need sensitive counseling to disentangle fact from fantasy, to do the letting-go work and to deal with the pressing problem that is giving rise to these hallucinations.

If the cause is due to some psychic ability to see into areas that are not permitted or to engage the place-memory phenomenon, then I would recommend that the person receive simple cleansing and freeing prayer. In this sort of prayer I would ask the person to repent of whatever psychic ability he has. I would then cut him free in Jesus' name from the effects of this ability and ask the Spirit of God to cleanse and renew him and heal any damage done. This is often quite a simple exercise, although if the person has had deep involvement in these things the process can be a long one.

In the case of place-memory phenomenon, some prayers may need to be said in the actual location of the ghost manifestation. For one reason or another there is an appearance, and even if it is a type of "photo," it is still a presence that does not belong in this world. It records perhaps a hurt from the past that has left its mark and may have power and influence on the living. It may not be scientific, but it is fact nonetheless that people are affected by "atmospheres," sometimes quite powerfully. In such a case, prayer for healing a hurt from the past would be appropriate.

In my experience, when the lives of those who have psychic ability come under the lordship of Jesus and the influence of the Holy Spirit, this ability becomes sanctified. These are often the people who are most open to the more intuitive gifts of visions, pictures, words of knowledge, etc.

If we discern that the haunting has a demonic origin, then deliverance ministry is appropriate and necessary. Deliverance prayers should be said by those experienced in that field.

Where the apparition is discerned as being actually the soul of the departed, then we need to discover the reason for the presence of this soul. He or she may be there in a type of angel-messenger ministry for some reason, expressly permitted by God to speak to the living. I am well aware that we are on somewhat shaky ground here, but I think that the way to test these things is to judge by their fruits. Take the case, for example, of the appearances at Medjugorje. Many Christians, evangelicals included, have flocked to this village to be present in the village church when Mary appears to the children there. The children claim that Mary speaks an evangelical message of repentance and exhorts her listeners to proclaim Jesus to a needy world.

If the fruit of this phenomenon is that a cult of Medjugorje is founded, in which Marian devotion replaces devotion of Jesus, then I would question the source of the visions. If, however, as seems to be the case at the moment, the fruit of the visions is a revival of faith in Jesus in a highly secular country, then I would probably want to say that God is always bigger than the little box we try to put Him into. If He chooses to bless people through this type of phenomenon, who are we to argue? It could be a case of "what God has cleansed, do not call common."

One regular experience of those who encounter renewal is to find that God, from time to time, has to lower a sheet before us of things that we had hitherto written off as unsound, "unblessable," useless to God. We have to repent of the judgments we have made and open our hearts to a new channel of God's blessing. Thus, someone from a house church might receive blessing through an Anglican Communion service; or an evangelical might discover a new depth of prayer through the rosary or benediction. And I for one want to be open to receiving blessings from the Lord however He chooses to give them. Having said all this, we cannot abdicate our responsibility to weigh and discern matters and to seek the truth in all things. In these days we urgently need the Spirit of truth that He may lead us into all truth. And note: The point of truth is not to lead us into legalism but to set us free.

Finally, a haunting may be due to the presence of the unquiet dead. It is to this subject that we turn in the next chapter. We shall find that there is a close connection between hauntings and hurtings—hurt not only in the living but also in the dead.

And what of my nighttime visitor? Just who or what was he? In this chapter I have presented possible options. As I said at the beginning, my conviction for many years was that he was a demon impersonation. I am now not convinced of that understanding and I am really too far away from the experience to come to an accurate conclusion. If it was the soul of some man who was a Quaker, a soul still trapped in this world, then I do pray that he will be released and that God will take his soul. How all this happens is the subject of our next chapter.

5

Healings and Requiems

In this kind of general prayer, therefore, 'for the faithful departed', I conceive myself to be clearly justified, both by the earliest antiquity, by the Church of England, and by the Lord's Prayer.

John Wesley[1]

The word *requiem*, according to the dictionary, means "a service, with or without music, for the dead." By this definition it could apply equally to an ordinary funeral service or a special occasion including the Eucharist.

I remember officiating at a funeral service at the crematorium in Bolton when I was a curate. As we came to the section in the service for prayers before the final committal of the body for cremation, I asked for a time of quiet. Then I said something like the following: "As we begin our prayers for Jack, it might just be that some of us are thinking, *If only I had known when he was going to die, I would have said this or that to him.* Or perhaps some of you would have done some special service or act of love for him. But because he has died you may be feeling that you are stuck with unsaid words or unfulfilled deeds. Well, through Jesus, you have an opportunity to offer Jack your words and deeds. So in the silence, open your heart to Jesus and through Him say those words you wanted to say, give those deeds you wanted to do. Let Jesus take your gifts and reach out in eternity and touch Jack with them, because God is the God of the living, both in this world and the next."

When the service was over, a number of people came up to me and said that they had followed my advice and found that, as they prayed silently, they felt that they had been healed of such things as migraine, arthritis and, in one case, angina. Their simple act of requiem had brought a measure of healing to their lives. This is not too hard for us to accept; many ministers could testify to similar happenings. It could be said that the mourners were enabled through prayer to redress or come to terms with their relationships with the deceased and ask forgiveness; the release that follows often results in physical benefits.

This testifies to the fact that we are a unity of mind, emotions and body. To receive blessing in one area of our lives cannot help but touch upon the other aspects also. Of course, the funeral service is also the time when we can commend the departing soul to continue its journey fortified by God's keeping love and power. Incidentally, when we are not certain or even if we know that the deceased was not a committed Christian and born again of the Holy Spirit, it is still incumbent upon us to be charitable toward the individual as we commend him or her to the issues of eternity. An early conclusion here, therefore, is that we can all be involved in requiem healing to some degree, simply by caring for the departed and underlining our respect and love for him or her in the funeral service we attend.

The issue of requiem healing can be taken much further, however, to incorporate ideas such as: releasing the departed from a kind of purgatory in order to enter heaven; healing the living from ills that were common to the departed; recognizing forgotten lives such as aborted, stillborn or miscarried babies; and breaking generational sins and curses that have come down the family tree to afflict the living. Perhaps the foremost practitioner of this developed approach to requiem healing is Kenneth McAll.

For the purpose of this book we shall be looking at Dr. McAll's approach to requiem healing and examining how it compares to our studies so far.[2] Dr. McAll came from a family of evangelical and non-conformist missionaries to China. His mother's family were members of the London Missionary Society and his father's background was that of Congregational preachers. Indeed, one of his relatives founded what is today the Protestant Evangelical Mission Church in France. He remembered as a child having family prayers and reading *Daily Light*.

As a missionary in China himself, he was challenged by the way an itinerant Chinese woman preacher delivered a man from demonic power in the name of Jesus. This brought the whole issue of possession to his attention. His studies, which included a degree in psychiatry, began to focus upon the relationship between the possessed mind and the resultant effect upon the body. He also noticed that some patients seemed to act out the illnesses that were known to afflict their deceased relatives.

In one case early on in his ministry he approached the suffragan Bishop of Ludlow, the Rt. Rev. Parkinson, for advice about a family he was seeking to help. He was quite surprised when the bishop suggested holding the requiem Eucharist for the deceased. He recalled that on the Monday when the Eucharist was held, his patient, who was in a padded cell in a London hospital, was healed. At the same time his patient's aunt, who was in a mental hospital in north Wales, was also healed. The actual diagnosis of his patient in London was that of hallucinogenic schizophrenia. Apparently she had an urge to gouge out people's eyes.[3] It seemed that holding a requiem Eucharist for a deceased relative who had similarly exhibited a form of schizophrenia resulted in the healing of such illness among the living. This experience was formative for Dr. McAll, who began to work almost exclusively through the vehicle of the Eucharist, which he suggested is the most powerful context for healing, both for the living and the departed.

THE POSSESSION SYNDROME

The states of possession that Dr. McAll first noticed in China, he found also in the United Kingdom. He was to define this term more precisely and suggest three forms of the possession syndrome: that of the living to the living, the dead to the living and the living to the occult.

1. Possession: The Living to the Living

We are all familiar with stories of people being in bondage to another person's will. The cases of the possessive parent who dominates the child either by sheer willpower or by "smother love" are well documented. Leanne Payne, in her book *The Broken Image*, suggests that one of the reasons for emerging homosexual behavior is the individual's response to this wrong kind of parenting. She explains how freedom and healing come when the domination is confronted and broken, and when, through the love of Jesus, the "injured" party is able to forgive the parent and choose to live more freely in God.[4]

In *Healing the Family Tree* Dr. McAll tells the story of Ruth, a mother who dominated her youngest child, Rufus. Rufus was eight years old when his father died. From then on he felt that his life was completely ordered by his mother. His choice of career and even of his wife were his mother's choices. His wife was in a sanatorium suffering from tuberculosis, and Rufus was a schizophrenic, confined to a mental hospital. The mother, on being challenged to face up to her domination of her son, was at first angry and stormed out of the consulting room. Later on, however, while she was in church, God challenged her to repent and to cut the umbilical cord to Rufus. She fell to her knees and said: "If this is true, Lord, I will do it now." Here is what happened, in Dr. McAll's words:

> On this fateful Thursday afternoon, Rufus had felt a sudden surge of release. He wrote immediately to his mother, telling her that 'he felt he was himself again' and that he had asked the hospital for permission to spend the next weekend with his

brother. Rufus was wholly cured. His wife also had felt unusually well on the same day and, after various tests had proved negative, was discharged from the sanatorium. . . . Twenty years later, Rufus and his wife are still fit and well.[5]

This form of healing and deliverance does not present any real problems to most of us. The ministry of inner healing has been adopted by many Christians over the last twenty years. The problems begin to emerge when the one who has exercised such domination over another is dead and apparently beyond our reach.

2. Possession: The Dead to the Living

This is by far the most controversial aspect of Dr. McAll's teaching on possession. He contended that the illnesses and disturbances, be they "ghosts" or "voices in the mind" that the living suffer, are due to the unquiet dead. He said that those who were unprepared for death

> can see that they are out of the body but do not know where they are. Because they are not committed and haven't had a funeral service, they are still earthbound. Therefore they are wandering and so look for family members through whom they can register their presence.[6]

He substantiated his belief with an impressive number of recorded case histories. His initial response was to construct a family tree of the patient and see if there were any similarities in the behavior of the living one who was distressed to the known behavior of the deceased. Next he looked for any cases of unprepared death in the family line. It seemed that the most common category for the latter is abortion, spontaneous or otherwise. Once the departed relative had been identified, a Eucharist was held in which the dead were named specifically and the need for forgiveness for them or the living was pronounced. In cases of anorexia nervosa, where the deceased person was so named, Dr. McAll cited an 85 percent success rate.

While the evidence of healing is substantial, his thesis contains some serious questions for us. First of all, is it true that the dead actually exercise some hold over the living? Could it not be demonic spirits at work or the projection of the troubled person who gives external reality to his or her inward hurt or sins? Dr. McAll was well aware of these possibilities, as we shall see in the next section.

It is a basic evangelical conviction that the dead reside in some place awaiting the judgment of God, places we might call paradise and Hades. Dr. McAll suggested that the dead do go to a place like purgatory where they need to undergo necessary cleansing and freeing from any unfinished business. The requiem ministry has the effect of releasing the trapped soul and enabling it to continue its journey toward heaven. We have seen that there are some grounds for this as far as the Christian dead are concerned.

The real difficulty comes with Dr. McAll's idea that such freeing and releasing into heaven is also true for the unsaved or uncommitted dead. Is this salvation after death? He referred to those who are somehow trapped as "lost souls" and distinguished between them and those who have damned themselves in whatever way such an action may be possible.[7] He was not clear about what this action is, but he stated that those who have died without commitment to Christ do find release through a requiem Eucharist and find their way to God. While he wanted to resist going down the road to universalism, he emphasized that God is as gracious to a person after death as He is before. I think that this is a necessary challenge to evangelicals who paint a picture of a God whose love has no further claim upon the lost when they die.

Still, while Dr. McAll acknowledged (quoting William Barclay) that the word *judgment* in the New Testament implies discipline rather than punishment, there was no escaping this teaching of Scripture: Without a commitment to Christ, death brings a prospect of spending eternity without enjoying the fellowship of God.[8] This is not to deny or undermine the healing that came to his patients, but it does show the great need to be cautious when making statements about how the deceased enter heaven. In the final analysis such statements cannot be verified and hold importance only for the individual concerned.

Dr. McAll, as well as some of his patients, reported seeing in a visionary way the deceased sharing in the Holy Communion service and going up into a great light. During one such requiem, he was puzzled to see a young airman called Keith, still in uniform, enter the church reluctantly. After reflecting upon the message of the Eucharist, he went up into a great light and looked peaceful. During a meal afterward Dr. McAll spoke to the mother who had requested this ministry for her eighteen-year-old son who was addicted to drugs. He asked her who Keith was. She grew agitated at this question and revealed that she had previously been married to an eighteen-year-old young man named Keith. He had been shot down over the Baltic ocean three months after their marriage. Only her husband knew of this; none of her children had been informed. Interestingly enough, the son had been going to the Baltic coast to indulge his drug-taking. He was healed as a result of this service and no longer resorted to the habit.[9]

This is, however, just the kind of visionary link[10] that gives rise to the speculation that this is simply spiritualism in another guise. Dr. McAll was specific when he said that this form of requiem healing is talking to the Lord about the dead and not talking to the dead. He never encouraged the living to seek contact with the dead. In fact, he believed that spiritualism is a great evil and opens the door to spiritual forces that bring harm to the living as well as to the dead.

Biblical evidence weighs heavily on the side of people speaking about their dead to the Lord. Daniel prays to God about the sins of their fathers, which led to their captivity (see Daniel 9:16). The psalmist prays to God that He will not hold the sins of his fathers against him (see Psalm 79:8). It could be said that the whole institution of the Day of Atonement hinged upon remembering the ill effects of the ministry of Aaron's sons Nadab and Abihu (see Numbers 3:4; Leviticus 16:1–34). The great prayer of the Levitical priests in Nehemiah is a conversation with God about the lives of Abraham and Moses and the disobedience of the rulers who came after them (see Nehemiah 9). Also Paul, then writing to Timothy, speaks of the apparently deceased Onesiphorus, that God would be merciful to him on the Day of Judgment (see 2 Timothy 1:16–18). On this evidence, then, we cannot say that requiem healing is spiritualism; it is, in fact, in keeping with the practice of both the Old and New Testament saints.

Some have questioned the validity of this form of healing because they do not believe that the living can be affected by the dead. There is, however, biblical evidence for this as well. A number of prayers and sacrifices deal with the need for deliverance from the sins of the fathers.[11] We have already referred to the subject of sins and curses being visited upon the generations and have seen that these are broken by asking God for release and forgiveness for the sins of our dead relatives.[12] I think it is also implicit in the death of Christ that when He died for the sins of the whole world, He made provision not only for our salvation but also for our deliverance from the sinful effects of those who have harmed us. Jesus offers us a salvation that leads to healing and wholeness.

We have discussed previously the fact that people can be affected because of abortion, stillbirth or miscarriage that has happened within the family. In the process of his work Dr. McAll concluded that in all these cases a real life has been lost and often feels rejected. Being nameless it does not feel part of the family to which it belongs. In addition, it is well documented that mothers suffer from guilt long after having had an abortion. The requiem offers a chance to say sorry to such a baby (through the Person of Jesus Christ) and then to name the child. In cases where the sex of the child is not known, then it is advised that the parents pray about this and proceed as they feel led. The release for the parents is often powerful and there can be dramatic healing also. Dr. McAll found that this form of requiem has the effect of recognizing, loving and accepting the forgotten or lost life. The following is a case history from my own involvement in requiem healing.

Frank was concerned for his 26-year-old son, Bob, who was living the life of a homosexual transvestite. Frank was a committed Christian and an elder in his local independent evangelical church. His son had left some years before to train as a chef. They had not really had a close relationship for some years. At the time when Frank requested my help, his wife had been dead for about six years. Bob had announced to his father that he was thinking of going to America with his boyfriend. (In his homosexual relationship Bob exercised the female role.) Frank feared he would lose contact with his son altogether, and it was this that prompted him to seek help. Frank was quite an outspoken critic of his son's way of life, but he did love his son even though he admitted not showing his affection adequately as far as his son was concerned.

When I met with Frank to discuss how to pray for his son, I asked him to give me a full account of the members of his family and anything that would throw further light on Bob's behavior. Frank told me that his son was a twin and that at the time of his birth it was discovered that the other child, a female, had died some time earlier during the pregnancy. I shared two thoughts with Frank in the light of this information. First, had he acknowledged his daughter, named her in the presence of God and commended her to the Lord Jesus?

Second, I asked him to consider the fact that during Bob's earliest moments of life he was intimately related with and connected to his sister. Then at some time during the relationship, which would include not only physical but also emotional dimensions, the female life he had known from conception had gone without warning and preparation. Surely this was bound to affect Bob at some level.

Frank went away to consider and pray about this and we met a week later. He told me that he had had a most moving experience of God's compassion and healing. While reflecting upon the fact that he had a daughter who would now be 26 years old, who was living in the presence of God and with whom he would one day be reunited in fellowship through Jesus, he broke down and wept. He realized that he had ignored, discounted as nothing, his own daughter who was made in the image of God. The memory also came back to him that he and his wife had always wanted a daughter and, if they had, they would have called her Mary after his wife. So as an act of faith, he repented of disowning his daughter, gave her the name of "Mary" and entrusted her to God. Frank said that although he had found the whole experience traumatic, he did feel that he had received an inner release that he had not known before.

Within a day or so Bob telephoned to say that he was no longer going to America. He went on to say that earlier that day he had been sitting in his flat preparing to leave when the door opened, or so he thought. But when he turned round he could see nobody, although he was sure he had felt someone come into the room. Then he felt that someone spoke the name "Mary" in his ear and he began to cry for no apparent reason. His crying, he later said, was a kind of release because from that moment he knew he was no longer homosexual. He cancelled his plans to go to America and eventually returned home to see his father.

Father and son were able to talk about their differences and find reconciliation. His father explained what we had shared, because Bob had never been told that he was a twin. It seems that Bob's sexuality had been confused because, after a time of complete harmony in the womb alongside his sister, she had died and something in Bob continued to look for her. It was only when his sister, Mary, had been recognized and named that Bob, who was at least two hundred miles away at the time, received his healing. Frank found that he could "step down" from his dominant approach to his family and open himself up much more to loving and being loved. He now enjoys his life as father and grandfather, and Bob has come to a real faith in Jesus Christ.

In these days of abortions "on demand," this kind of healing is needed more and more. I am quite sure that such a dispatching of innocent lives leaves its mark of disquiet and dis-ease not only upon the lives of those who make such decisions but also upon the hospitals that carry out such operations. I have been in conversation with a number of doctors and nurses who report that such hospitals seem to have more than their fair share of mismanaged operations (in other departments) and often seem to carry a depressive atmosphere—so much so that many of the staff prefer to work elsewhere. In several of these places some of the Christians have begun to pray for the aborted lives and ask God's forgiveness. They report improvement in working relationships and other results as a consequence.

We should not underestimate the value of naming these children before God. In doing so we are recognizing that they are real people who really live, even though they did not enjoy a proper birth and life. Consider the fact that we name our children at baptism or dedication services and pray over them and commit them to God's keeping care; such an act is meant to bond the child to Christ, his church and also the child's family in faith. Names are powerful factors in a life. Zechariah is struck dumb when he argues with God about the arrival and naming of his son, John, known as the Baptist.

Neither should we be in doubt that children are real, even though they were aborted or miscarried. After all, Jeremiah receives his prophetic call in his mother's womb (see Jeremiah 1:4–5); the unborn John the Baptist, upon hearing his mother speak of the Christ to be born of Mary, responds with his own witness of joy and is filled with the Holy Spirit even from birth (see Luke 1:15, 39–41). Esau and Jacob are engaged in a struggle for supremacy within their mother's womb; they "fell out" before they "came out" (see Genesis 25:21–26). And if this were not enough to convince us, the psalmist speaks of his formation within his mother as being under the daily supervision of God, who sees and nourishes the life within (see Psalm 139:13–16).

Whether or not we can substantiate accounts of these "forgotten" children being released and going on to heaven in some way, requiem healing is nonetheless a service we must render to them, as well as to those who lost them, if we are to cherish life from God's perspective.

3. Possession: The Living to the Occult

Before examining the requiem service itself, we must give some consideration to the suggestion that we may not be dealing with the dead but the demonic. It is quite probable that the sources of family information at seances and the like are not dead relatives but demonic forces impersonating the dead in order to deceive and ensnare the living. Raphael Gasson tells of a time when he challenged the alleged spirits of his dead ancestors who were his "spirit guides," for he was an accomplished medium.[13] He was rudely awakened to the fact that these spirits were, in fact, demonic and that he needed deliverance from them in order to walk properly with God. For a more complete survey of the occult world and directions for bringing deliverance to such people, see my book entitled *The Occult: Deliverance from Evil.*[14]

Dr. McAll was well aware of the possibility of the demonic and so suggested that as a matter of course, with any request for healing, a careful study be made before engaging in ministry. This would include a full medical investigation, as some forms of alleged demonic activity may, in fact, be depressive psychosis, schizophrenia or the projections of a troubled mind. (The normal procedure in the United Kingdom when one is not sure of the problem is to recommend a consultation with a psychiatrist who is sympathetic to the deliverance ministry.) This is not to rule out the fact that, given such medical problems, there can still be the influence of the demonic. Dr. McAll noted that the test for demonic presence is the patient's response to prayer and to the Eucharist. Even the offering of silent prayers can cause an erratic response within the patient, and this is a good clue to the need for deliverance from the demonic.

Often there will be a need to break demonic heredity in the family. Some years ago I was asked to help a member of a church who was suffering from attacks of violence and rage out of all proportion to his circumstances. Stephen reported having involuntary trances and hearing voices; at the same time he always felt as if someone was placing a hand upon his head. He had received a lot of prayer counseling but the problems persisted.

As we discussed his problems we discovered that his grandmother was a medium. When Stephen was born she had prayed over him to receive her "psychic gifts." Healing and deliverance only happened after he renounced his grandmother's involvement in the occult and asked for cleansing and deliverance in the name of Jesus Christ. There were no further manifestations from that time onward. Dr. McAll cited with approval a prayer by Kurt Koch that he found helpful when delivering people from the bondage of the occult: "In the name of Jesus Christ I renounce all the works of the Devil together with the occult practices of my forefathers, and I submit myself to Jesus Christ, my Lord and Savior, both now and forever."[15]

A further contribution to this discussion on family history and the demonic is that of "spirits of the dead." Sometimes a demonic spirit that has had a hold on a dying person attaches itself to a living relative at the time of death. If evil spirits can attack us through the living, as in the example of the man called Legion or the abortive episode of the seven sons of Sceva, then it is equally likely that such spirits can attack us through the dying who may have been similarly demonized.

This would accord to some degree with Dr. McAll's assertion that when there has not been proper Christian preparation for death and committal to God after death, then the deceased becomes an easy target for demonic attack. In some cases the demonic spirit reproduces the personality of the deceased and so brings the living into a kind of bondage to the dead. When a person feels dominated by a parent, therefore, even though that parent is dead, there may well be a need for deliverance from a spirit of domination rather than just inner healing from the effect the parent left upon the child. Granted there is little biblical documentation for this idea, but the subject deserves discussion. At the very least it serves to underline the importance of proper preparation and prayer for the dying. It also serves as a reminder to include some general prayer of deliverance when seeking to bring healing to any relationship between the living and the dead.

Finally, we need to touch upon the whole area of ghosts and hauntings as well as the possibility that the problem is one of projection by the sufferer. It is possible that some of the problems we feel about the dead are the projected hurts we feel inside. Very often, if we feel guilty about the way we treated someone who has died, we may imagine that we see that person haunting our lives. Dr. McAll said that ghosts are issues of human form that we do not want to face. He cited the example of the woman who might see in dark doorways figures of men intent upon rape; this happens because she so fears and denies her sexuality that her feelings are projected outward. Ghosts may well appear as lustful figures.[16] He suggested that one way to minister to this, far from denying her "ghosts," would be to hold a Christian service for "whatever may be there." This allows the person to forgive whatever she cannot face and so switch her focus to Jesus and overcome her fear. Such an approach helps the person to become reconciled to that part of him- or herself that has been denied.

More and more Christians are coming to realize nowadays that most ghosts are not necessarily demonic or projected images but the distressed dead who have somehow become trapped upon earth. This is usually because the death of the person concerned was unplanned—as in the case of murder, death by disease or war—or there were no proper funeral rites or prayers of committal. This means that they are distressed and in need of some direction. It is up to us as Christians to declare the lordship of Christ over their presence and over their problems.

Far from needing the ministry of deliverance, then, what is more appropriate is some form of requiem healing. Such a service is the fulfilling of what was denied to them by virtue of their unprepared deaths. Most evangelical ministers when officiating at a funeral service include some form of prayers for the departed that commend them to the peace of God. It is not for us to make decisions about whether they were truly converted or not. In the final analysis only two people really know how a person stands with the Almighty—the individual concerned and God Himself. A requiem service, therefore, offers those prayers of committal that have gone unsaid for however many years since the person died. Surely if we feel it proper to pray for the departed at funeral services a few days after their deaths, then praying for them many years after death is a crossing of the same divide.

I well remember listening to an edition of "Woman's Hour" on Radio 4 some years ago. It dealt with the visit, the first by any pontiff, of Pope John Paul II to the site of the death camp of Auschwitz in Poland. The woman reporting on the visit said that it was a place where no bird sang nor plant grew. The feeling from the horrific deaths of millions hung like a dark shadow over the place. Imagine the change when, on the very day that the pope celebrated the Eucharist and related the death of Christ to the slaughter of millions of his fellow countrymen, the birds began to sing and the whole atmosphere changed. No doubt this is a very subjective observation, but it speaks powerfully to the need to bring the death and resurrection of Jesus Christ to the many who have died without being remembered. This is why the ideal context for a requiem healing is the Eucharist, the breaking of bread.

REQUIEM HEALING AND THE EUCHARIST

The practice of holding services for the dead in combination with the Holy Communion is an old and well-attested practice of the Christian Church. The writings of Teresa of Avila, Thomas Aquinas, Bernard of Clairvaux and Elizabeth of Hungary all refer to the healing power of the Eucharist both for the living and for the dead. Matthew and Dennis Linn mention in their book Bernard's account of how St. Malachy held a series of requiem Eucharists for his dead sister. The two had not gotten on well for some years.

One night Malachy dreamt of his sister standing at his door in need of food and refreshment. When he awoke and reflected upon his dream it occurred to him that the food she needed was the living bread of Jesus Christ. So he held a number of Communion services for her until in his dreams he saw her now released from her poor state and in the blessing of God.[17] Whatever substance we wish to give to his actions and convictions, we must note that the saint also received healing, because he at last came to terms with his sister. We need to keep in focus that in the final event, the requiem must be for the benefit of the living.

Dr. McAll advised that we need to decide who, apart from the minister, should be present at the service. Whenever possible it should include the living persons in need of prayer, as they can use the occasion to accept Jesus Christ's love for themselves as for their deceased family members. Other loving friends or family who wish to pray or who are prepared to be open to the love and power of God in Jesus should be invited. He suggested beginning with informal prayer in which God the Father is asked to call out to the dead who live before Him and enable them to witness the acts of love and confession that are to take place.

He divided the requiem service into four stages from this point.

1. Deliver Us from Evil

Using the Lord's Prayer to begin the service, we ask God to free both the living and the dead from any bondage to the evil one. As the Eucharist focuses upon the blood of Christ, represented by the wine, such deliverance is inviting the Lord Jesus to cleanse the bloodlines of the living and the dead of all that blocks healthy life. This would include breaking hereditary seals and curses by casting out any evil spirits. We have already examined the subject of how demonic spirits can attach themselves to families down through the generations; beginning any requiem service in this manner is a way of opening all the needy areas to the lordship and power of Jesus Christ. This often helps to release more of the healing power of the Holy Spirit for the benefit of the living.

2. Forgiveness

It is vital that the living let go of any resentment, hurt or guilt that makes them hold on to or be held by the departed or the demonic. Dr. McAll went further and said that in the requiem, forgiveness is offered to the departed. He underlined the familiar words of the eucharistic prayer, which, in speaking of the blood of Christ, say "which was shed for you and for the sins of many." The "many" include the living who have never received Christ's forgiveness and the departed who may never have been told of God's love for them in Jesus. He also said that the Eucharist offers a double forgiveness, as it includes an opportunity to ask the departed to forgive us. Many a mother has come to this place and, through confession to Jesus Christ, has asked forgiveness from the children whom she has aborted or of whom she took no notice because they were miscarried early in the pregnancy. Certainly when we ask for forgiveness it is like letting go of issues we have either denied or held on to for years. It can bring great relief and healing as well as lead us to the place where we can hold a better and more positive relationship with that person.

Some time ago I led a group of street evangelists in a biblical meditation where they were encouraged to imagine themselves walking down a sort of Emmaus road. They were to choose any road they knew and then after seeing themselves walking along it, Jesus would come and join them. Here they were to share with Him any issue that concerned them and then listen to what the Lord would give them in exchange. At an appropriate moment they were to go and share with another what the Lord had said to them.

Almost a year later I was sitting in the team lounge at the Spring Harvest event in Minehead when one of these evangelists came up to me and shared what the exercise had meant to her.

As soon as she closed her eyes she found herself in a wooded clearing near a town she knew well. In the clearing she found Jesus, and with Him was a young, playful boy. As she looked Jesus said to her, "This is your son, R—. I want you to know that he is in My care, but you can play with him for a few moments before I take him home with Me." The young boy duly ran to her and she held him in her arms and loved him and wept. The woman went on to tell me that she had had an abortion some years before and had never felt free enough to tell anyone. The guilt had left a scar on her emotions that prevented her from really entering into all that the Lord had for her. But now she felt full of joy because Jesus had her son and he was growing up with the angels. She said that she had been forgiven and was free to go forward with God for the first time in years.

3. The Offering

Dr. McAll placed great importance upon this moment because it is a sharing of and witnessing to the offering of Christ's death and resurrection: "Whenever you eat this bread and drink this cup, you proclaim the Lord's death until he comes" (1 Corinthians 11:26).

During this part of the service the people concerned are encouraged to place their family trees or the written names of people for whom they are specifically praying or even gifts and tokens of love for the departed on the table along with the gifts of bread and wine. This is a good suggestion because it helps us to see our giving in the light of the gift of the Son of God for us all. It is an opportunity to name the individuals for whom we have come to pray. In doing so we recognize their right to live and give dignity to their persons, especially if this was denied to them in their deaths. It is at moments like this that death wishes are broken, such as in those suffering from anorexia nervosa. They are given space at the requiem to offer love and forgiveness to the one they miss so much. It is a way of saying goodbye and saying: "You are now in your rightful place in my heart."

Many taking part report at this point seeing their deceased relatives entering into the joy and peace of Christ. These are purely personal visions and should be kept as such, but it is interesting to know that they do not lead to attempts to hold on to the dead or to communicate with them afterward. The whole point about requiem is that the living and deceased have come to terms with each other through Christ, and so there can be a letting go of the dead into the hands of God.

4. The Blessing

Here we see the focus shifting from the needs of the dead to those of the living. It is an opportunity to lay hands on them and pray silently or otherwise for them to receive whatever healing God wishes to give them. It is also an opportunity for anointing and for the signing of the cross. Here we can turn fully to Jesus and offer ourselves for His service now that we have been released and renewed. We can move on from being bound in an unhealthy way to the past and go forward in the power of the Holy Spirit. As the final words of the Eucharist rite in *Common Worship* exhort us, we are to:

Minister: Go *in peace to love and serve the Lord.*
People: *In the name of Christ, Amen!*

We pay tribute in this book to Dr. McAll's pioneering work in this field. He was largely criticized and dismissed for his ideas during the bulk of his lifetime. With the passage of time, however, many have come to recognize their debt to his work even though they may not agree with all of his ideas.

Before asking ourselves what differences requiem healing can make to our Christian lives we must see if a model for this kind of ministry can be found in the Bible. It seems evident that Jesus offers just such a model, and He demonstrates it when He finds friends in a cemetery.

6

Jesus, the Model
for Requiems

*Jesus called in a loud voice, "Lazarus, come out!" The
dead man came out. . . . Jesus said to them, "Take off the
grave clothes and let him go."*

John 11:43–44

The purpose of this chapter is to offer a biblical outline for
an approach to requiem healing. We have discussed in some
depth the whole issue of relationships between the living and the
dead and reviewed a particular approach to requiem ministry.
Now we need to find a way in which we can benefit from this
ministry while retaining our commitment to the Word of God.
In the beautiful story of Lazarus being raised from the dead,
we find that Jesus' healing touch gives life to the mourners as
well as to the departed. Jesus' ministry to the grieving family
offers us three principles that we can incorporate as we engage
in the need for requiem healing. They are as follows:

Listening to the wounds
Ministering to the departed
Restoring the relationship

LISTENING TO THE WOUNDS

When Martha and Mary hear that Jesus is outside, they rush to Him and share their hurt. They both give a voice to their pain and anger when they say, "Lord, if You had been here, my brother would not have died." They seem to imply that Lazarus should not be dead and that if Jesus had been present He could have healed him and prevented this. Perhaps this is a clue as to how unprepared they were for the death of their brother.

Jesus, upon hearing their story and seeing their distress, is moved deeply and weeps Himself. What a tremendous contrast this is! He who is the Resurrection and the Life stands by a tomb and weeps. This should encourage us to share our hurt feelings with Jesus about our departed. It is good to know that His resurrection life and power do not hush our crying. Similarly at funerals and requiems Jesus gives us space to share with Him our hurt about the departed. He listens to our wounds.

It is also a place to share our hopes for the departed. Martha and Mary both look forward to seeing Lazarus again on the day of resurrection. They will see him then free of his ills and in full vigor of life. A requiem gives us the opportunity to share our hopes that our departed will be healed of their ills and enjoy the Kingdom life of God in eternity. The following is a summary of some of the wounds that we might be carrying either about or from the departed.

1. Unprepared Deaths

Here we are thinking primarily of those who had little or no opportunity to prepare their souls for death and leaving their family and friends. These deaths are due to such things as accidents, acts of violence as in war or murder, unforeseen illnesses and suicide. Not only might their wounds need to be brought to Jesus, but very often the living can also be suffering shock or guilt from their sudden removal.

I remember praying with a friend whose father had died quite suddenly when he was only seven years old. Three months later his mother committed suicide and so he was brought up by a distant aunt. Years later he still had feelings of being abandoned and felt overcome by the temptation to give up on life when it became difficult.

As we prayed for his parents, suddenly a "picture" came forcibly to his mind of his father in the hospital in which he had died. Jack was actually out of the room when his father died, but in this picture he saw Jesus help him climb onto the bed with his father. His father hugged him and said how sorry he was to be dying as he felt he had not given enough love and affection to Jack. Jack had been given a vision-picture from Jesus to help him see by faith the healing journey that he was experiencing. He told his father that he had always thought he had died in order to get away from him. Now he knew his father loved him, and he thanked Jesus for giving him this insight. This experience also became the springboard by which he could appreciate his mother more completely and accept her death, tragic as it was. Jesus had brought Jack to a place where he listened to his wounds.

2. The Unquiet Dead

As we have noted, these are spirits of the departed who have been unable to find their proper place of rest and seek to bring this to the notice of the living. They can be members of our own family from past generations or people who are attached to the place of their death or suffering. Here we need to do our homework. Provided that we are satisfied that such happenings are not demonic in origin and are sure of the identity of the departed, we need to bring their wounds to Christ. We speak on their behalf rather than just our own.

3. The Forgotten Dead

Here we are re-owning as ours and God's those lives that were aborted or lost through miscarriage. There is also an opportunity for the ones responsible for abortion to repent, receive forgiveness and be released from the effects of the guilt they have been carrying. There can be space to apologize through Christ to our children for rejecting them and not recognizing them as ours, made equally as ourselves, in the image of God. It can be liberating to know that the children we forgot have not been forgotten by God and that in due time we shall all be together with the Lord.

4. The Wounds of the Dead

Here we are dealing with the sins, curses or afflictions that have come down the generations of a family. Sometimes the bondage of evil spirits needs to be broken from our families in order that the living may go free. To facilitate this we may need to repent on behalf of our ancestors. This is perfectly in order when we consider that the great saints of the Old Testament often prayed for the sins of the nation and their forefathers. People like Ezra, Jeremiah and Daniel often prayed, "O Lord, forgive us for we have sinned." We know already that they had not rebelled in the way that the nation had, but they still included themselves and identified themselves as being equally responsible before God.

Also, the Lord's Prayer reminds us that we need to forgive others their trespasses against us in order for God to forgive ours. This passage needs to be understood in two basic ways. First, it refers to the way in which we may be holding on to bitterness and grievances due to how folk have sinned toward us and hurt us. It is as if our lives are full of the consequences of unforgiveness and God cannot find room to give us His healing. Those whom we need to forgive can be the dead just as much as the living. When we let go of the issues we have been nursing and keeping alive within our hearts, then, and only then, do we find that we have space to be more open to God and enjoy His forgiveness and blessing.

A second approach to this part of the Lord's Prayer is that of bringing the sins of our departed dead to Christ and asking His forgiveness in order that the consequences of these ancestral sins may be broken and removed. Where there has been involvement in the occult, for instance, there is often a history of mental and emotional stress in the descendants. Prayers of deliverance, which can come only when forgiveness has been received, often result in the hurting family being delivered of demonic influence and healing taking place.

Sometimes when there has been deep shock or hurt in a family, it can have far-reaching effects upon succeeding generations. I remember, some years ago now, being asked to pray for a man who was afraid that the "family curse" was going to catch up with him. He described how the men in his family had had an almost continuous history of mental illness, which afflicted them around their fortieth year.

Through prayer and sharing it came to our knowledge that almost a hundred years earlier one of his great-grandmothers, when pregnant, had witnessed a brutal stabbing. She was so shocked by the event that she went into labor and gave birth to a baby boy. Apparently the mother was in her early forties when this happened. In subsequent prayers and ministry, intercessions were offered for the moment when mother and son were in shock, with the request that the effects of this experience be removed from the rest of the family. Not long after this time, both the man's father and grandfather improved so much that they were discharged from the mental hospitals where they had been. He himself is happily married and enjoying life in his forties.

It is certainly true that we shall not be judged by the sins of our forebears but, as the word *atonement* implies, we may need to have the effect of such sins or curses lifted from us. Thank God He has provided a place for us at Calvary where we can come in faith and offer sins! We know they will be removed because Jesus died not only for our sins but for the sins of the whole world (see 1 John 2:2).

We join with Jesus, therefore, when we listen to the wounds that the living may be carrying about their dead and, having listened, we take the next step: engage in the appropriate ministry.

Ministering to the Departed

Having been deeply moved by the love and pain He sees at Lazarus' graveside, Jesus then turns His attention from the living to the dead and says, "Take away the stone" (John 11:38). Martha immediately reminds Jesus of the finality and fruits of death; her brother's body has been interred for four days and the decomposition will be quite marked. Yet the subject of death is no barrier to the power of Jesus Christ; He enters in where we fear to tread.

The removing of the stone tells us that there is no blockage of access for Jesus: Here He enters the realm of the dead some time before He goes and preaches to the imprisoned spirits in Hades (see 1 Peter 3:19; 4:6). Another important factor is that Jesus goes to the place of death and brings His healing. This was to prove vital and true for His own death. This means that we can go with Jesus to the place of death we are considering in our request for requiem healing—not necessarily the actual grave, but by faith into the time, the issues, the place. And because Jesus is the Resurrection and the Life, the most suitable context for this ministry, though by no means the only one, is Holy Communion.

There are a number of reasons for the appropriateness and the power of such prayer within the Communion service. Here we focus on the twin issues at the heart of the Eucharist: proclamation and remembrance. Paul says that participation in the Lord's Supper is a way we "proclaim the Lord's death until he comes" (1 Corinthians 11:26). So Communion becomes a visual demonstration of Christ's death and resurrection to all.

This theme is picked up in the liturgy of both the Anglican and Roman Catholic rites. The Proper Preface to the Sanctus says: "Therefore with angels and archangels and all the company of heaven, we proclaim your great and glorious name. . . ."[1] Here the living and departed, alike and together, proclaim—to all who will hear—the greatness and the majesty of the Lord Jesus Christ. The proclaiming of the name of Christ moves on to proclaiming "his mighty resurrection and glorious ascension."[2] We can complete this idea of proclamation by looking to the words of Paul in Ephesians, where he says that "through the church, the manifold wisdom of God should be made known to the rulers and authorities in the heavenly realms" (Ephesians 3:10). The Eucharist is one of these moments when the Church, together with the heavenly host, declares the wisdom and the power of the cross to all the powers and authorities.

Also at the core of the Eucharist is the value of remembrance. Jesus encourages us to take part in this celebratory meal in remembrance of Him. So we remember a particular death at this table of the New Covenant. Because we are allowed to reach back and touch the death of Christ, so, through Him, we can touch those deaths in our families that are significant for us. We can say to the deaths that have touched us deeply that here is another death, more powerful in its effect than theirs. The healing effects of Christ's death, therefore, can overcome whatever ills or hurts these other deaths may have brought.

In remembering our departed, we can say that the death of Christ and the shedding of His precious blood were not only for the forgiveness of our sins but for their sins, for the sins of the many. So we identify ourselves with the healing of the cross and proclaim it to be more powerful in its effects than any issue that has hurt us from our departed dead. We can also proclaim that healing was offered for them, and leave the consequences of such witness to the faithful working of the Holy Spirit.

To summarize, we can say that the Holy Communion is the best context for requiem ministry because:

it proclaims the power of Christ's death;

it proclaims God's offer of salvation;

it proclaims deliverance from demonic power (see Colossians 2:15);

it proclaims God's offer of forgiveness for all.

RESTORING THE RELATIONSHIP

After Jesus calls to him, Lazarus comes out from the tomb, with all the trappings of death upon him. So Jesus instructs his friends to take off the grave clothes and let him go. It is not enough to bring him back to the world of the living; he needs to be given back his family.

This is always the touchstone of whether or not requiem ministry has been properly completed. The living come to a place where they have a proper relationship with their dead. In the case of Lazarus it was restoration to life and renewal of his place alongside his sisters in his home. While we cannot usually expect a rising from the dead, we can hope for a renewal in the way the living will now be able to relate to their dead relatives.

The Lazarus story tells us that God does want to restore a true and proper relationship between us and our departed. Suppose, for example, we are asking God to forgive us for forgetting or treating as nought a miscarried life or an aborted life. Then in recognizing the dignity of that person we have brought ourselves back into a proper relationship with him (or her). We hold him in our hearts and, if he is already in God's Kingdom care, then we have God's Word to assure us that on the last day we shall be together with the Lord forever (see 1 Thessalonians 4:16–18).

If we have been remembering those who were ill-treated, killed violently or who carried great hurts, then in requiem we are saying that we recognize their right to life and that Jesus' offer of healing is equally for them. As to the consequences for their lives in eternity resulting from this action, it is not for us to say. We offer them to God and accept that they are ours, they are part of our family, and we can go on into our future safe in the knowledge that we have been released from any hold or effect that they may have had upon us.

Requiem healing helps to create, by the grace of God, an appropriate relationship with our departed. Because of this, the departed are much freer to go on into what God has for them.

We can now conclude that requiem healing offers a biblical model for healing help for both mourners and departed alike. In the next two chapters we will explore how this ministry impacts our approach to giving pastoral care to those who want healing for their own grief and loss or who recognize the need for generational healing for their family stories.

7

Requiem Healing
and Pastoral Care

If we adopt the views that we have expressed in this book, what difference does it make in our walk with God and the way we care for His people? Both of us have been involved in pastoral work for many years, and we both share the same concern that what we write should not be theory for textbook study, but should be something that can be worked out in life. In this chapter we suggest a number of ways of working it out.

GIVING PEOPLE PERMISSION TO LOVE THEIR DEAD

Part of the great pain of grief is that sense of the enormous gulf that separates the living from the dead. In the case of a sudden death, the bereaved will often say, "He was there one minute, and the next he was gone." And this will be said not only with great sorrow but also with great puzzlement, because there is something so very mysterious in all this. It has something to do with the mystery of people going somewhere, yet without their bodies. It is somehow "spooky" and altogether rather frightening. And in a way one wonders if they are still going to be friendly in their new condition and place.

"But where are they?" is an often-asked question. C. S. Lewis expresses this so well in *A Grief Observed*, when he asks this question about his recently deceased wife, whom he refers to as "H":

> 'Where is she now?' That is in what place is she at the present time? But if H is not a body—and the body I loved is certainly not she—she is in no place at all. And the 'present time' is a date or point in our time series. It is as if she were on a journey without me and I said, looking at my watch, 'I wonder is she at Euston now?' But unless she is proceeding at sixty seconds a minute along this same time line that all we living people travel by, what does 'now' mean?[1]

There is a sense in which activity in the next world will always be a puzzle to us—and thank goodness for that or it would be a great disappointment! But this sense of distance is not helped by our taking a rigorous separatist view of the dead. If a man has loved his wife for 45 years and one day she is suddenly in a different world, he does not stop loving her. Indeed for the believer it would be a sign of weak faith to stop loving her, because that would imply that she no longer exists, which, in Christ, she does. But how does he show his love for her? Obviously he can no longer cuddle her, bring her cups of tea, talk to her, listen to her, walk with her and do all the thousands of things that communicated love in this world. He has to find a new language of love that can communicate to her world.

And this, of course, is the great attraction of spiritualism. There is no doubt that spiritualism meets this need, though through totally unchristian and deceptive means. But the reason spiritualism has thrived is because the Church has had very little to offer the bereaved. Yet Christian hope has so much to offer! We are permitted to love our dead, just as the early Christians did—as is revealed in the tomb inscriptions mentioned in chapter 3. It is true we cannot engage in conversation, and we cannot do all the things that meant so much to us here in this world. But now part of us is in heaven, and we have to use heaven's ways of expressing our love. Prayer for the dead, in the sorts of ways that we have discussed in this book, is simply a way of expressing our love for the departed.

Adrian Plass writes movingly about Bishop George Reindorp, whose baby daughter, Veronica Jane, died suddenly at an early age. George Reindorp was enormously comforted by a letter sent to him by a good friend. The letter includes this passage:

> It has been given to me to see our progress to God as a road divided in the middle by a low wall, which we call death. Whatever our age or stage of development, or relationship with other human beings, there is no real change involved in crossing the low wall. We simply continue in a parallel course with those who loved us in our development and relationship. I do not believe that God altered one whit your responsibility or service for your child.
>
> I do believe that she will grow side by side with you, in spirit, as she would have done on earth; and that your prayer and love will serve her development as they would have done on earth. There is nothing static about the other life. . . . The companionship which was given you, you still have. The growth to which you look forward will still be yours to watch over and care for.[2]

George Reindorp was given permission to continue to love his daughter in her death, and for him this has been a source of great healing.

Making Sense of Post-Death Meetings

It may have come as a surprise to some readers to learn that post-death meetings, where the recently departed makes a sort of return trip to speak to the living, are not uncommon. Here are three examples, one from a book I read a few years ago, and two from my own pastoral contacts (whose names I have changed).

Bob. In 1987 Bob Jackson wrote a moving account of the death of his son, Matthew, and the subsequent journey of grief that he, his wife, Christine, and their daughter, Ruth, had to take. Matthew was a lively ten–year-old boy who died from a fall while the family were on holiday in Austria. Ruth, Matthew's older sister, was also involved in the accident and had to spend some time in the hospital recovering. It was during her early days in the hospital that she had this experience:

> When Ruth awoke about an hour later her face had miraculously changed and cleared. She looked serene and was smiling. 'God and Matthew have spoken to me', she said to Christine who was with her. 'It wasn't a dream, it was much more than that. They were real and they were outside me. God held my hand tight. I could really feel it. Matthew said to me, "You are safe and I am safe, so why worry?"'
>
> 'And what did God say to you, my love?' Christine asked.
>
> 'He said, "I love Matthew even more than you do, and I want him with me now"'.

Ruth was to know many ups and downs in her adjustment to bereavement, but that encounter was her turning point. A few pages further on in the book Bob Jackson writes:

> Christine's father cried over Matthew each morning for several days until he heard what seemed to be his voice simply saying, 'Don't cry Poppa'. What are we to make of these things? Perhaps Matthew was allowed to help us in our time of need.[3]

Brian. Brian is a friend and a member of a church I belonged to. His wife came to church regularly but Brian only occasionally. In the winter of 1988, his father became ill and died after Christmas. Brian went over to the family home in Wales for his father's last days, and he was with him when he died. Soon after his father had breathed his last breath, Brian went downstairs and sat in the familiar chair in the familiar room but being terribly conscious of the absence of his dad, whom he loved. It was in these moments of quiet, on his own, that he suddenly became aware of the presence of his father. It was more than that experience commonly felt in the early stages of bereavement. It was like a visit, and his father spoke to him and reassured him.

For Brian it was a life-changing experience. Not only did it provide him with a profound sense of comfort, but it also convinced him of the reality of the afterlife and the existence of God. He came to see me a few days after this experience and since then his faith has been very important to him.

Mary. Mary lost her mother shortly before Christmas 1989. In the New Year she wrote to me and told me of this experience. Although her mother had been unwell, her death was unexpected and Mary was taken into deep grief. But in her letter she writes of how she was comforted:

> However, on the next day, as I walked from room to room I found myself looking for someone, or looking to see what this person was doing. Then later I understood. I was upstairs sorting clothes when I suddenly felt love burning into me and something in me recognised my mother—not as she had been in the last few months, but as she was when I was very young. It was someone I had forgotten. She felt young—and free. The next morning—just fleetingly really—I experienced another feeling of freedom and gladness about being free of responsibility. Afterwards I wondered why I hadn't said various things to her, but then I realised none of this happened in my brain. I shall treasure the memory of the love she gave to me at that moment. It was quite in character for my mum. She would have thought that she hadn't thanked me for the last few months and that she hadn't said she loved me—neither of which I would have expected but which nonetheless she would have wished to have said. Neither would she have wanted me to worry about her, hence the statement of how she was. It certainly made the

funeral much easier and I really felt that the coffin had nothing in it that mattered any more.

These are experiences of three different people, and there are thousands more who would testify to similar experiences. A few years ago I would have questioned their theology and would have felt distinctly uncomfortable with them. Now I feel I understand a little more clearly what is happening. The wall is lower than I thought, and such is the greatness of the Lord's compassion and love for us that He will permit His saints to have these post-death meetings. As usual, some discernment is needed, as some people who claim to have such meetings are experiencing more of a hallucination than an actual meeting. The test is the fruit of such a meeting. If the persons are moved on in the process of bereavement and their walks with the Lord become deeper as a result, I am inclined to believe the experiences as not only genuine, but also willed by God.

INNER HEALING

Inner healing is now a regular part of many churches' healing ministries. Those who are involved in inner healing will know that many people suffer because of their relationships with close family or friends who have died. The death of a friend or relative does not remove the hurt of a relationship that needed healing. Suppose, for example, a son has for many years been unforgiving toward his mother. While his mother is alive he has a chance to offer her forgiveness and seek reconciliation. There is always the hope for healing. But what happens when she dies? I have led many a funeral service in which there was a bad atmosphere because of unresolved family hurts and conflicts. The problem is, once the relative has died it seems that there is apparently no hope for reconciliation.

From time to time I have counseled those who are holding within them powerful feelings of hurt and unforgiveness toward a relative who has died, sometimes many years ago. What do they do with this? A number of us are used to working with a counseling therapy known as "gestalt." When appropriate in a bereavement situation, we actually get those being counseled to imagine that the deceased relatives are sitting before them. They then address them and speak out all that they are feeling. This is a completing work, doing that which the persons have been longing to do for some time, to work out of their systems the bad feelings that have been in them and to speak out their hitherto unexpressed good feelings. I have seen powerful results from this type of counseling and inner healing.

You could take this process just one stage further. Take the above example again. The son has unresolved feelings within him about his deceased mother. He wants to forgive her and get rid of the burden of guilt and the feelings of hurt within him. The gestalt work may well help him, and he could also be encouraged to speak out his forgiveness to his mother in her world beyond the grave. If we are right in believing that the wall is not quite so high as we thought, this spoken act of forgiveness will be heard in paradise. The son will have a powerful experience of having spoken out his forgiveness and a knowledge that his mother has heard. This would most appropriately be done in a prayer time, and the counselor would then want to bring the good news of forgiveness and healing to the son.

As we have seen in chapter 5, some inner hurt may well be due to the active presence of a departed soul interfering in a person's life. In our inner healing ministry, therefore, we will want to be open to this dimension and minister to it accordingly.

THE AUTHORITY OF THE CHURCH OVER THE DEAD

The gospels frequently emphasize the authority of Jesus. In the first chapter of Mark's gospel we hear of the crowds being amazed by Jesus because He taught with an authority that the scribes and teachers of the Law did not have (see Mark 1:22). This comment by Mark is followed immediately by the incident of the demonized man in the synagogue, and Jesus deals with him with consummate authority (see verse 25). The authority of Jesus is seen in His words and His deeds. It is emphatic and definite, and He asserts His authority over Satan, who is "the prince of this world."

It is, therefore, not surprising that this authority extends to death and the world of the dead. It is with this authority that He calls back Lazarus. His voice, used in this world, is heard by the discarnate spirit of Lazarus who is somewhere in the next. Because Jesus' authority reaches beyond the grave, the spirit of Lazarus has to obey. He returns to his body and is raised back to life. Jesus hands this authority on to His disciples. Thus, in the Acts of the Apostles we find the disciples operating in the power of the Spirit and exercising this authority (in the name of Jesus) over sickness (see Acts 9:32–35), nature (see Acts 16:25–28), demons (see Acts 16:16–18) and death (see Acts 9:36–43).

Peter was present when Jesus raised Lazarus and, having learned from Jesus, he is given his turn at doing something similar (see Acts 9:36–43). He is called to the home of Tabitha who has died. Interestingly he is asked to come "quickly" to the dead Tabitha, probably reflecting the Jewish idea that the spirit remains close to the body only a short while after the death. Their expectation is that, if Peter comes in time, the discarnate spirit will still be near enough to hear and respond to Peter. It all speaks of remarkable faith and confidence in the power and authority that they see in Peter.

When Peter arrives he sends the others out of the room (perhaps he learned this from the raising of Jairus' daughter), and he falls to his knees in prayer. I wonder what he prayed in those moments, kneeling beside the body of Tabitha. My guess is that he was spending time listening to God, discerning whether or not it was God's will for her spirit to be returned to her body. Having discerned that this was what the Father willed, he works with it. With a word of command he says, "Tabitha, get up," and she opens her eyes and is back alive again.

We are hearing nowadays a number of accounts of people being brought back from death. I was recently at a conference in London where a man was present who had been working in a village in South Africa. He had been used by God to call a woman back to life. I did not meet this man, but I met a close friend of his who verified the story. It takes a lot of discernment to know whether or not it is appropriate to pray in this way (not to say a fair bit of courage!).

In his book *Power Healing*, John Wimber has an interesting section on death. In it he discusses this idea that Christians need to discern the right time for death (see Ecclesiastes 3:2). He illustrated this by writing about an occasion when he was called to a hospital to pray for a baby who was critically ill:

> When I entered the baby's room, I sensed death, so I quietly said, 'Death get out of here'. It left and the whole atmosphere in the room changed, as though weight were lifted. Then I went over and began praying for the girl. . . . Within twenty minutes she was improved greatly; several days later she was released completely healed.[4]

On arrival at this hospital room, John Wimber clearly discerned that this was not the time for death and accordingly took authority over it.

We should also note the rather disturbing incident in Acts where death actually occurs as a result of the authority of the apostles (see Acts 5:1–11). However we understand this rather strange story of Ananias and Sapphira, it is clear that the Church is given authority that extends to death itself.

The Church is, therefore, given authority to operate in the name of Jesus, who is the Resurrection and the Life, and this extends to the realm of death. What does this mean for us? There are two pastoral implications:

Ministry to the Dying

This is a highly delicate area in which good pastoral practice is essential. Every situation will be individual and different. There will be some occasions where the corporate sense is that the person concerned is dying, and what is needed is appropriate pastoral care for the person and the family. There may also be occasions where there is a strong corporate sense to continue to pray for healing. Such discernment can be difficult, though in my experience I have found that it will be made fairly clear how we should pray. God, the lover of souls, is more committed than we often realize to lead us at times like this and to make the way clear.

Twice I had the privilege of being part of an anointing service for Brother Ramon SSF. The first occasion, it was clear that the anointing and prayers were to be aimed at health and recovery, despite the fact that there was a fairly grim prognosis. Ramon did recover well, and for over a year he enjoyed good health. Not long before his death, however, he asked us to gather again. This time the anointing was not to be for restoration to health but for the fuller healing of Sister Death. Both services were authentic expressions of the healing ministry, and both were rooted in careful listening to Ramon, the community and to the Holy Spirit.

When we feel led to pray for the journey of death, then this is the time for the church to gather around—not to pray for recovery but to take its authority, to entrust the dying to God and to send them on their way. Jesus entrusted His spirit to God at His death; we follow the same principle by entrusting the spirits of our loved ones to God at their deaths, that they may journey from this world to the next. The next chapter offers some prayers for this ministry. Also there are a number of prayers in the Church of England Pastoral Services. [5]

The Funeral Service

In my early days of taking funerals it used to strike me as slightly odd that I never addressed the deceased directly. We all talked about him and referred to him, but in a way we tried to pretend that the coffin was not there. The funeral service is often seen as a farewell to the departed, only the departed is not actually part of it. We deal with the body, but we are not sure what we are doing with the spirit. If we acknowledge that we have been given, in Christ, authority over the dead, then we will have a "higher view" of what takes place at a funeral. This service has, I believe, a very important role in actually committing the departed to God. In committing the departed to God we are not assuming that his or her destiny is paradise. We are committing the person to God for Him to determine where the person should go. By doing this we are making it clear that this world is no longer the person's home.

I make use of a prayer (see the next chapter) that makes clear that I am committing the deceased to God, telling the individual to leave this world and go on to the next. In this way, I feel I am taking up my authority appropriate for the occasion, and I am making sure that there is no danger of the spirit remaining in this world, causing distress through ghost phenomena. In this way I am ministering to the departing spirit, not to the congregation. What always has to be borne in mind, of course, is that, in a folk religion culture, language of this sort may well encourage a belief in universalism. Ideally, therefore, there will need to be included in the service some reference to judgment and our accountability before God. It is not an easy path to tread!

8

Remembering and Releasing

The acts of remembering and releasing are fundamental to our faith. The act of worship that Jesus institutes with His disciples on the night of His betrayal is an act of remembrance. There was nothing strange for the Jew in being told to remember something significant. All their lives, the disciples had been at religious family meals where remembering the great saving acts of God was at the heart of the event. And so, at the Last Supper, Jesus offers the bread and the wine as symbols of His body and blood and tells the disciples to "do this in remembrance of Me."

Releasing is also important in our faith. Jesus spoke to Peter, the man who was going to lead the infant Church, telling him, "Whatever you bind on earth will be bound in heaven, and whatever you loose on earth will be loosed in heaven" (Matthew 16:19). When He appears to His disciples in the Upper Room following His death and resurrection, He breathes on them the Holy Spirit and speaks about releasing people from their sins (see John 20:23). Jesus gives His Church the authority and the power to be involved in a ministry of releasing people from chains that bind them.

This chapter offers suggestions for prayer that can be used in situations such as healing Eucharists, funeral services, prayers at home, visits to the bereaved and also following counseling or grief therapy. Some are to do with releasing the dead and some with remembering them. There is nothing particularly sacrosanct about any of the prayers; you might want to adapt them and personalize them in appropriate ways. We do not claim any particular literary merit for the ones we wrote—they are simply here to give you an idea of what you can do.

FOR THE DYING

Into Thy merciful hands, O Lord,
we commend the soul of this Thy servant
now departed from the body.
Acknowledge, we meekly beseech Thee,
a work of Thine own hands,
a sheep of Thine own fold,
a lamb of Thine own flock,
a sinner of Thine own redeeming.
Receive him into the blessed arms of Thine unspeakable mercy,
into the sacred rest of everlasting peace,
and into the glorious estate of Thy chosen saints in heaven.

Bishop Cosin, 1160–1174

Remember Your servant, O Lord,
according to the favor that You bear unto Your people
and grant that, increasing in knowledge and love of You,
he may go from strength to strength
and attain to the fullness of joy in Your heavenly Kingdom,
who lives and reigns in you and the Holy Spirit
now and forever. Amen.

Liturgy of the Episcopal Church of Scotland

Dearest Lord,
You know how we have loved _____ in life.

Watch over her soul now as she prepares to embark on the
   Great Journey
where she will be more fully in Your presence
and alive in your love and joy.
Guard her in her traveling,
bring your full healing to her,
and watch over all of us during the sad time of parting.
Plant in our hearts the good seeds of hope;
we ask in the name of our Savior Jesus. Amen.

Addressed to the dying person:

_____, the Lord your God has given you life.
You are a part of our hearts,
we will always hold you dear.
Yet now your time has come
and we release you into the tender care of the Good Shepherd.
Depart from this world, but not from our love
in the name of Christ our Lord. Amen.

MAKING USE OF ALL SOULS' DAY

It is the custom in many churches to send letters to all
those who have been bereaved during the past year to invite
them to come to an All Souls' service where their lost loved
ones will be remembered. This has all sorts of pastoral and
evangelistic benefits, as many of the bereaved will make their
way back into church for the first time since the funeral.
The point of a service like this is to remember the deceased
before God in a way that affirms the love that the bereaved
had for them. Permission is given for weeping and feelings
of loss, as the house of God is a safe place for offering grief
and sorrow. But it is also the occasion for releasing—releasing of memories of the funeral and a further releasing of the
deceased into death.

The following is an example of a prayer that might be used
on an occasion like this.

Gracious Father,
at this festival time we rejoice together in the glorious hope
    of resurrection.
We thank You for all who have gone before us
and we remember today those whom we have lost during
    this past year.
We offer You now our love for them,
our memories of them,
all the joys and the sorrows that we shared
and the grief of recent days.
Give us we pray further strength to face the future and the
    assurance of life eternal. Amen.

FAMILY PRAYERS

Most families have experienced bereavement. In the case of
a family where a beloved relative has died in Christ, there may
well be something very right and therapeutic about remembering the person on the anniversary of the death, as the early
Christians were accustomed to doing. Suppose, for example,
a grandmother has died and it is known that she died putting
her trust in God. The family may want to have a short service
on the anniversary of her death. Readings can be chosen from
1 Corinthians 15 and other suitable passages—perhaps the passage that was used at her funeral. Hymns and songs could be
sung that speak of God's comfort and the promise of heaven.
The family could make use of symbols such as candles, flowers
or other signs of resurrection. Then there might be prayers for
Grandmother such as the following examples.

Lord Jesus,
You are the Resurrection and the Life.
We thank You today for the life of _____
and for all that she meant to us in her life here on earth.
We now remember her
and pray for her that she would know our love
and would be enjoying all the joys of heaven.

Help us to follow You as she did.
And we rejoice in the hope that one day
we shall walk with her in paradise. Amen.

Lord God of the endless age,
who holds all life in the palms of
His hands;
we come to remember and celebrate
_____ whom You hold in keeping care.
We miss her.
The gifts of her life we carry still.
Through our Lord of heaven
we want to say "Thank you, _____,
for all you are and gave to us.
Rest in the peace of Christ until
God brings us all together again." Amen.

PRAYERS OF GOODBYE AT A FUNERAL

As mentioned in the last chapter, the funeral is a crucial time both for committing the departed soul to God and for saying our farewells. The following is a prayer that could be used at a funeral to help the mourners express what may be going on inside of them.

Loving Father,
if only I had known when _____ was going to die.
There were some personal words I would have shared and
some things I should have done with him
and some things we had yet to do together.
But I missed the opportunity.
Yet, Lord, I do rejoice that You are the God of the living and
of the dead.
In Your presence, therefore, I share with _____ my unsaid
words and my unfulfilled deeds.
"_____, through Jesus Christ, hear my words and receive
the
things I would have done for you."

(In a time of silence share your own thoughts with your
loved one.)

> Father, I thank You for this opportunity to share my heart
> with _____ through Jesus Christ, Your Son.
> I now say farewell and release _____ to You.
> Keep him in the knowledge of Your love;
> bring him joy and peace and the assurance of our love for
>   him,
> through Jesus Christ, the Resurrection and the Life. Amen.

Some people may like to use the prayer Newman uses in
"The Dream of Gerontius," where those who represent the
Church on earth commend the departing Gerontius to God.
The words have been updated and used as follows.

> Go forth upon your journey from this world, O Christian
>   soul.
> In the name of God the Father almighty who created you,
> in the name of Jesus Christ who suffered death for you,
> in the name of the Holy Spirit who strengthens you,
> in communion with the blessed saints,
> and aided by angels and archangels,
> and all the armies of the heavenly host.
> May your portion this day be peace,
> and your dwelling the heavenly Jerusalem. Amen.[1]

Where the faith of the deceased is not known, here is a more
general prayer:

> Go forth from this world, O soul,
> to that place appointed you by God;
> in the name of the Father who created you,
> and in the name of Jesus Christ who died for you,
> and in the name of the Holy Spirit who gives life to the
>   people of God.
> May the light of God go with you as you journey from this
>   world,
> and may you rest in peace. Amen.

Circle _____, Lord
Keep hope within, keep doubt without
Circle _____, Lord
Keep light within, keep darkness out
Circle _____, Lord
Keep peace within, keep fear without
Circle us, Lord
Keep hope within, keep doubt without
Circle us, Lord
Keep light within, keep darkness out
Circle us, Lord
Keep peace eternal within, keep fear without.

Miscarried Pregnancy and Stillbirth

At whatever stage a child is lost, an appropriate time of entrusting the child to God will be of great help to the parents in the grief process and will ensure that the life of the child is indeed entrusted to God. There will be times when the sex of the child is not known, though very often the mother has an intuition about this. These are highly sensitive occasions and require great tenderness. The parents will usually know if they want to name their child. It is sometimes the case that either you or the parent will hear the Lord speak a name, which makes this service very special.

Dear Father, we are hurting because the baby we were look-
ing forward to so much has died/been lost.
We feel empty and numb and deprived of this precious life.
Part of us is still looking for her, and search as we might we
cannot find her.
Yet Lord, we know that she is safe with You because You
love and cherish every life.
You said, "Let the little children come to Me," and so we
bring our little daughter to You.
We want her to have the name _____.

Let _____ know that she has parents who love her and
long to meet with her again in the garden of paradise
when our family will be truly complete.
We entrust _____ to You and ask that she may grow in
grace and in the knowledge of our Lord Jesus Christ.
Amen.

or

Almighty and heavenly Father,
we thank You that we are all created in Your image and
share Your likeness.
We bring before You our child who was not able to be born
into this life.
In faith we name her _____ and commend her to Your
keeping.
We rejoice that she is going to be brought up by Jesus together with the angels who worship You.
We look forward to that time when we shall all be together
at the coming of our Lord Jesus Christ. Amen.

PRAYERS FOR ABORTED LIVES

In our experience many parents, particularly mothers, find
a need for prayer and committal to God of a life they lost
through abortion. It is difficult to find a prayer to suit everyone,
because it is always going to be such a personal experience. In
this prayer we are assuming that the parent wants to express
sorrow and is seeking forgiveness. It is a prayer of releasing the
soul of the child and of releasing the parent from guilt.

Most gracious Father, I ask Your forgiveness for my sins and
especially I am sorry that the life of my child was taken
through abortion.
I am grateful, Lord, that You do know all about the pres-
sures, the difficulties and the problems that caused me to
make that decision.

Whatever my reasons, Lord, I am truly sorry for the taking
of this life.

I ask forgiveness from You and from my child who has died.

I take this opportunity to acknowledge before God that I do
have a child and recognize him as my own.

Please receive this child into Your care, and assure him of my
love.

In faith I name him _____ and I look forward to that day
when, through faith in Christ Jesus, we may be reunited in
paradise. Amen.

Prayers for Forgotten Children

In our experience it is quite common to find that parents can
become acutely aware of a child they lost through miscarriage
or abortion many years after the event. Grief that has been
trapped inside for a long time finds its way to the surface and
breaks out, and the parent recognizes the existence of another
member of their family. At an appropriate time during the counseling process one of the following prayers may be helpful:

Dear Lord Jesus,

You were always glad to be in the company of children and
taught us that we must be like them to be in the Kingdom
of heaven.

As parents, we now realize that we have more children in our
family than we first accepted.

The child who was lost through miscarriage is also ours.

We are sorry that we have forgotten and ignored him and we
ask his forgiveness and Yours.

It helps us to know that no child is lost to You.

In faith, therefore, we now name our child _____ and ask
You to heal him of any shock or hurt that he has carried
as a result of the way he died.

Heal the hurt between us, and join us now as one family.

Thank You, Jesus, that You died and rose for our child as
well as for us, and so we trust that through the coming of

Your Kingdom in glory, we shall see him and be restored
to each other. Amen.

Loving Father,
We pray for any children today who were miscarried or
aborted.
We ask You to heal their scars and draw them close to You
where they will always abide in Your love and healing.
Set them free from any shock or hurt that may be preventing
them
from being fully at peace in Your Kingdom, so that they may
joyfully dwell with You in paradise.
Through Jesus Christ our Lord, Amen.

PRAYERS FOR THE UNQUIET DEAD

We offer here two prayers for use in situations in which
a member of the family has died and is still trapped in this
world.

Both prayers ask God to take the soul away from this world
to the next. We do recognize that in some cases the eternal
destiny of the soul will not be known. In the prayer we express
our hope that the destiny is heaven, but we leave the judgment to God. These prayers are requests to God. Should you
want to use a prayer that involves a direct command to the
deceased to leave this world, then you could use one of the
funeral prayers above.

Dear Father,
In seeking Your healing for our home and family, we have
learned of the damage done to (by) _____ who is our relative.
We pray in the name of Jesus that You will now remind her
of the victory of the cross of Your Son, Jesus Christ, who
died that we might be free from sin and be healed.
We pray that whatever sin or problem has tied her to us will
be healed now.
In the name of Jesus we cut ourselves free and entrust her
soul to You.

Bring her Your peace and mercy. We express before You
our hope that she will enter Your Kingdom and be kept
safe until the day when Christ comes again as Savior and
Mighty Conqueror. Amen.

The following prayer is useful where a particular problem
that is besetting a member of the family is seen to be similar
to one of a departed family ancestor (alcoholism, depression,
etc.). Here we break any unnatural tie and say a prayer of release for the ancestor in case that spirit is still having an effect
on the living.

Heavenly Father,
We have learned that the need we see in (A) [the afflicted
family member] is the same as that of our departed
ancestor (B).
In Jesus' name we cut (A) completely free from any influence
of (B).
By Your blood shed on the cross have mercy on this family.
Deliver us from the sins of our forefathers, and remove any
harmful influence from our family.
We commit to You the soul of (B) and ask that You would
now receive him to Yourself.
We ask this in the name of Jesus our Lord, who is the Resurrection and the Life. Amen.

BREAKING BONDAGES OVER GENERATIONS

If a particular bondage has its origin and influence back one
or more generations, the following type of prayer will bring a
great release. The prayer is in three parts: The first proclaims
the liberating work of Christ and expresses the situation
before God; the second is a deliverance prayer that sets free
the afflicted; the third is a prayer of healing. Because this is a
deliverance prayer it is essential to have someone present who
is experienced in this type of ministry.

We thank You, heavenly Father, that through the death and
resurrection of Your Son, Jesus Christ, You have conquered all
the powers of darkness and set the captives free. In the name
of Jesus Christ we now stand against the unclean spirits that
have had their influence down through the ages and are now
holding _____ in bondage.

In the name of Jesus we say to these spirits: "We break
your power over this family and command you to get out. We
forbid you to have any more hold over _____ and deny you
all access to him. We proclaim that the blood of Jesus Christ
was shed for _____ and all his family, bringing healing and
cleansing from sin. Go from this family to that place appointed
for you by God, and we forbid you to return. In the name of
Jesus Christ who is Lord of all life."

(You may find you need to continue this stage further, re-
peating this prayer or using others until you are satisfied that
the deliverance is complete. Then continue with the prayer
below.)

We thank You, Father, that You have broken this bondage
and have brought freedom and deliverance to _____. Now
strengthen and heal him. Free him to walk in newness of life,
that he may grow daily in the power of Your Holy Spirit,
through Jesus Christ our Lord. Amen.

The *Church of England Common Worship* Pastoral Services
offers a large range of prayers for the time of a death including
collects, thanksgiving prayers, prayers for those who mourn,
prayers after a short life, after a sudden death, after a violent
death, after a suicide, after a long illness, in sorrow, guilt and regret, litanies, commendations and blessings.[2] These services can
also be found at: www.cofe.anglican.org_/commonworship

Conclusion

May the LORD *do so to me and more also if even death parts me from you.*

Ruth 1:17, RSV

"The Lord bless him! . . . He has not stopped showing his kindness to the living and the dead."

Ruth 2:20

The subject for heated debate on the television program "Friday Night Live"[1] was that of death and survival beyond the grave and whether or not there are any legitimate means to maintaining a relationship with the dead. Various mediums extolled the virtues of their craft while the Christian belief in the death, resurrection and lordship of Jesus Christ was firmly represented by the Rev. Graham Dow, formerly rector of Holy Trinity Church in Coventry and now the Bishop of Carlisle.

The debate was aired in response to a film entitled *Ghost.* Basically the story line is that of a young man who is suddenly killed and who, because of the shock and impact of his own death, is unable to leave his familiar surroundings to go to heaven. He finds that he cannot tell his fiancée how much he loves her, although he is present with her as she tries to come to terms with the tragedy. What was significant about this film was that it attracted millions of young people to watch it and became a box-office success.

While not wishing to endorse the spiritualism portrayed in the film, for reasons already stated in this book, there are some factors underlined in the film that are of real concern for Christians. First, the subject is of sufficient importance to draw large numbers of young people who, it may be reasonable to assume, have not lost a loved one but for whom survival beyond this life is important. Second, the central message of the film is the idea that both the living and the dead do not stop loving and caring about each other after death has occurred.

The fascination with this theme persisted through the film media with the blockbuster *The Sixth Sense*. In this story a young boy of nine keeps seeing the dead but does not know why. The heart of the film brings him the answer to the mystery: The dead are carrying hurts and unfinished business that they want the living to appreciate. Apparently only this small boy is sensitive to this. When he discovers this is the reason for his experiences he loses all his fears and accepts his role as someone who helps the departed to be healed so that the living can get on with their lives.

The whole purpose of this book is to affirm that because Jesus is Lord of the living and the dead and holds the key to a salvation that extends beyond this present world, it is only in Him that these concerns find healing and fulfillment. The grief process, although it follows a defined pattern, is nonetheless a very personal journey.

GRIEF AND HEALING

For many people, problems with the grief process happen because they have not been able to let go of the deceased. Whether this is a case of projecting hurt feelings or the fact that somehow the dead have been prevented from completing their journey, it is good to know that through Jesus Christ there can be healing and letting go of the departed. It is perhaps important at this stage to suggest that not only the living but also the departed experience bereavement. Sheldon Vanauken was comforted by this thought when he shared his feelings of loss with his friend and mentor, C. S. Lewis.

> He [Lewis] was thoughtful about the idea of the dead undergo- ing bereavement. . . . [O]ne of us suggested that if the dead do stay with us for a time, it might be allowed partly so that we may hold on to something of their reality.[2]

He goes on to share how Lewis stated that in our journey toward the Eternal Being there is a necessary element of be- reavement and that this matches Jesus' words when He said, "It is expedient that I go away."[3] Vanauken endorses the need to hold on to the departed but says that eventually God brings us to the "Christ place" where we allow them to go away, hav- ing understood that, because we have been shaped by those we love, we hold a deposit of their lives within us.

For others, grief comes as a rude awakening as they realize that a miscarriage or an abortion involves a real life. Bernadette Thompson, a care assistant with mentally handicapped adults in Halifax, has shared how she was in a self-destructive state following an abortion. She says, "I fooled myself into thinking it was just a mass of cells. . . . [I]t was not until years after the abortion that I was able to face up to what I had done and then realise what I was suffering from was grief. I was mourning my lost baby."[4] She goes on to explain how the guilt in her destroyed her two marriages and that she was unable to find peace until she received Christian counseling. Although pain- ful at first, for Bernadette it came as a healing experience to realize that she was indeed grieving for a lost life. Through the resurrected Christ we can proclaim that although some lives have been lost to us, they have not been lost to God, and that at the final resurrection we shall all be together at the coming of Christ (see 1 Thessalonians 4:15–18).

A final area we have considered in the subject of grief is that of the ongoing distress or sorrow of the unquiet dead themselves, those commonly called "ghosts." This is brought to our attention either by the presence of unexplained phenomena such as noises, tapping, opening and closing of doors even when locked or by sightings of the dead who seem preoccupied or distressed. Such reporting does need careful checking in order to eliminate any subjective projecting of the individual's own concerns and worries. If there has been a resorting to spiritualism, this needs to be repented of and renounced in the name of the Lord Jesus. If after such precautions, however, the phenomenon does seem to involve some form of unquiet death, then what is needed is the healing of the death and not the ministry of exorcism.

Duncan and Joyce Wainwright have recently published a pamphlet entitled *The Great Release*, which details an account concerning the appearance of a maid in one of the rooms of a Christian conference center in the Midlands. Various prayers of deliverance had been offered by a former minister but to no avail. Duncan and Joyce, along with another minister and a female parish worker, decided to conduct a form of the Lord's Supper in this room and did so in May 1990. They felt that they were declaring to this maid that the Lord Jesus had died for her sins and that, because of this, they wished to point out that her personal sorrow or sins were all laid on Jesus. It must be stressed that such prayers are not a claim to offer salvation after death but to show the unquiet dead that Jesus is Lord of their times and, in so doing, release the departed from this world into the next. As a consequence of their prayers and recognition of the deceased, the Wainwrights reported that all the disturbing events ceased from the building and that there were no further sightings of the maid; a calmness and a lightness returned to the center.

In this book we have tried, further, to underline that a Christian response to these "unquiet deaths" is not to dismiss them as so much speculation but to bring the lives and deaths to Jesus, who by nature of His eternal being has access to all life both in this world and the next. Jesus is the true healing presence and is uniquely qualified to bring a proper fulfillment to their grief and ours.

As in the circumstances of Martha and Mary, when a death has influence over our lives, Jesus comes to our unresolved needs, shares our feelings and, at the same time, says that He is the Resurrection and the Life. Jesus commanded that the stone blocking Lazarus' exit from the tomb be removed. In a similar way, He enables us to speak to the mountains that block our way forward in life and see them removed.[5] This is not a pretext for spiritualism but rather an encouragement to bring to Jesus those we have not yet been willing to let go of, those forgotten deaths of our miscarried children or the unquiet deaths that exert undue influence over our lives.

THE RIGHT ATTITUDE

In concluding this book we offer some thoughts that may enable us to have a more fulfilling attitude toward those we love but, for the moment, see no longer. First of all, we see that it is perfectly acceptable to love our dead. We need, consequently, to be sensitive to people undergoing bereavement and not hurry them through the experience. The time for full letting go must be approached without undue pressure or strain.

Secondly, we need to be open to the fact that death does not mean that we cease to be, or that we are incapable of still growing. Those forgotten lives from miscarriage or abortion, for instance, have a future life in the presence of Jesus. The fact that such lives are growing up in the presence of Jesus offers us an opportunity to ask for forgiveness both from God and from the children themselves. Bernadette Thompson said that her life really began to find healing and peace only when she asked the child whom she had aborted for forgiveness for what she had done.[6]

Thirdly, we have noted that sometimes the illnesses and issues that dominated the lives of our departed relatives can become our troubles, too. Through the power of Jesus Christ, however, we can bring to God the sins of our forefathers and find healing and release for ourselves.

Finally, we have underlined the importance of the Eucharist as a context for requiem healing. It is this sacrament that speaks most powerfully about the death and resurrection of our Lord Jesus. It is only Jesus' death that can speak healing to the death with which we may be dealing. His death tells us that He can go down into all our unquiet deaths and say, "Peace! Be still!" The resurrection of Christ from the dead proclaims that death no longer has the last word. Similarly, the deaths that have been holding us so powerfully have to yield their power up to Christ, who will set us free.

Christ has died, but now He is risen and, therefore, death shall no longer have dominion over us.

> "Death is swallowed up in victory."
> "O death, where is thy victory?
> O death, where is thy sting?" . . .
> Thanks be to God, who gives us the victory through our
> Lord Jesus Christ.
>
> 1 Corinthians 15:54–55,57, RSV

> *Christ has died!*
> *Christ is risen!*
> *Christ will come again!*

Notes

Introduction

1. Kenneth McAll, *Healing the Family Tree* (London: Sheldon Press, 1989), 3.

2. Michael Mitton, *The Quick and the Dead*, Pastoral Series (Cambridge: Grove Books, 1987).

Chapter 1: Feelings for the Dead

1. Quoted in Judith Cook, *An Accident Waiting to Happen* (San Francisco: HarperCollins, 1989), 6.

2. Quoted in Jim Graham, *Dying to Live* (London: Marshall, Morgan and Scott, 1984), 150–51.

3. Elisabeth Kübler-Ross, *On Death and Dying* (London: Tavistock Publications, 1973).

4. Quoted in an anonymous article, "Obituaries and Pastoral Care," *Journal of Pastoral Studies* 98 (1989): 28.

5. Maxine Negri, "Age Old Problems of the New Age Movement," *Humanist* (March–April 1988): 23–25.

6. Raymond A. Moody Jr., *Life After Life* (Covington, Ga.: Mockingbird, 1975). See also Maurice Rawlings, *Beyond Death's Door* (New York: Nelson, 1975), which describes how the author's skepticism about Christianity and the need to be personally converted is deeply challenged by the resuscitation stories of his patients.

7. Matthew and Dennis Linn with Sheila Fabricant, *Healing the Greatest Hurt* (Mahwah, N.J.: Paulist Press, 1985), 181–82.

8. Rawlings, *Beyond*, 7.

9. *Church of England Newspaper*, 1 December 1989.

10. Jean Darnell, *Heaven Here I Come* (n.p., 1974), 35–44.

11. Duncan Munro, *Sickness Unto Death*, Ethics Series, no. 30 (Nottingham, England: Grove Books, 1989), 8. Words in brackets are mine.

12. Sheila Cassidy, *Sharing the Darkness* (London: Darton, Longman and Todd, 1989), 59.

13. Amy Carmichael, *Fragments that Remain*, ed., Bee Trehane (London: SPCK Triangle, 1987), 145. Quoted by permission of the publisher.

Chapter 2: Meeting with the Dead

1. Paul applies exactly the same description of Lordship over the living and the dead to Jesus Christ (see Romans 14:9).

2. A Hebrew term, which is translated "grave," "hell" or "pit" in the King James Version.

3. See Job 10:22; Psalm 88:12; 94:17; 115:17.

4. See Isaiah 14:9–11; Ezekiel 32:17–32.

5. Other Old Testament references to a hope beyond the grave include Job 19:25–26; Psalm 49:15; 73:24.

6. See also Matthew 9:24; 27:52; John 11:11–13; 1 Corinthians 11:30; 15:20, 51.

7. Quoted in William Barclay, *Death and the Life to Come* (London: Hodder & Stoughton, 1988), 615.

8. William Temple, *Readings in St John's Gospel* (London: Macmillan, 1949), 226–27.

9. Ibid., 227.

10. J. Norval Geldenhuys, *Commentary on the Gospel of Luke* (London: Marshall, Morgan and Scott, 1971), 615.

11. See 2 Corinthians 5:8; Philippians 1:23.

12. See Exodus 22:18; 2 Chronicles 33:6; Isaiah 2:6–9; Micah 5:12; Nahum 3:4.

13. Alexander Maclaren, *Exposition of Holy Scripture*, vol. 3 (London: Hodder & Stoughton, 1905), 376.

14. See 1 Samuel 16:14; 18:10–11, 20–21, 25; 19:1, 15; 20:30–33.

15. *Wilmington's Guide to the Bible* (Wheaton, Ill.: Tyndale House, 1986), 107.

16. John J. Davis, *The Birth of a Kingdom* (Winona Lake, Ind.: Brethren Missionary Herald, 1970), 96–99.

17. J. C. Ryle, *Expository Thoughts on the Gospels* (Cambridge: J. Clark, 1954), 205.

18. Alexander Maclaren, *Matthew*, vol. 1 of *Exposition of Holy Scripture* (London: Hodder & Stoughton, 1905), 347–48.

19. H. A. Ironside, *Commentary on Matthew* (Downers Grove, Ill.: InterVarsity Press, 1985), 210–11.

20. R. T. France, *Tyndale Commentary on Matthew* (Downers Grove, Ill.: InterVarsity Press, 1985), 262.

21. Alexander Maclaren, *Exposition of the Gospel of Luke*, vol. 3 of *Exposition of Holy Scripture* (London: Hodder & Stoughton, 1905), 546.

22. John H. Hampsch, *Healing Your Family Tree* (Performance Press, 1986).

23. Matthew and Dennis Linn with Sheila Fabricant, *Healing the Greatest Hurt* (Mahwah, N.J.: Paulist Press, 1985), 42–49.

24. William Barclay, *Daily Study Bible: Hebrews* (Edinburgh: St. Andrew's Press, 1976), 172.

25. Alexander Maclaren, *Hebrews*, vol. 12 of *Exposition of Holy Scripture* (London: Hodder & Stoughton, 1910), 167.

26. Ibid., 168.

27. *The Speakers' Bible: Hebrews* (Speakers' Bible Office, 1931), 319.

28. See Isaiah 24:21–22; 2 Peter 2:4; Revelation 20:1–7. See also William Barclay, *Daily Study Bible: James, Peter* (Edinburgh: St. Andrew's Press, 1976), 236–37; also E. C. S. Gibson, *The Thirty-Nine Articles* (Methuen, 1912), 159–65 for a description of the intermediate state of the saints in the Old Testament. The 1553 form of Article III reads:

"As Christ died and was buried for us; so also it is to be believed that he went down into hell. For the body lay in the sepulchre until the resurrection, but his ghost departing from him was with the ghosts that were in prison or in hell and did preach to the same, as the place of St Peter doth testify."

29. *New Bible Dictionary* (Downers Grove, Ill.: InterVarsity Press, 1970), 1212.

30. For the term *pneuma* to describe human personality, see 2 Corinthians 7:1; Colossians 2:5; for human perception, see Mark 2:8; Luke 1:47; 1 Peter 3:4.

31. Barclay, *Hebrews*, 241.

32. Mentioned by Gibson, *Articles*, 169.

33. Mentioned by Leon Morris, *Commentary on Corinthians* (Downers Grove, Ill.: InterVarsity Press, 1983), 218.

34. William Barclay, *Daily Study Bible: Corinthians* (Edinburgh: St. Andrew's Press, 1975), 153.

Chapter 3: Prayers, Purgatory and Protestants

1. *The Authorised Daily Prayer Book of the United Hebrew Congregation of the British Commonwealth of Nations* (London: Eyre and Spottiswoode, 1962), 431.

2. Josephus, "Discourse to the Greeks concerning Hades."

3. I am indebted here to a pamphlet by Michael Rear entitled *Praying for the Dead* (Church Literature Association), which records these inscriptions. His source is H. P. V. Nunn, *Christian Inscriptions—Texts for Students* (London, SPCK, 1920).

4. Quoted in Peter Brown, *The Cult of the Saints* (London: SCM Press, 1981), 106. His reference is Jerome, Ep. 103. 13.

5. E. L. Blant, *Les inscriptions Chrétiennes de la Gaule*, vol. 1 (Paris: Impremière Imperiale, 1856), 240.

6. Clement, *Stromateis*, 7:6.

7. Augustine, *De Civitate Dei*, 21:13, 24.

8. Brother Ramon, *Fulness of Joy* (London: Marshall Pickering, 1988), 205.

9. Jim Graham, *Dying to Live* (London: Marshall, Morgan and Scott, 1984).

10. Jesus uses the term *asleep* to describe the condition of Jairus's daughter before He raises her (see Luke 8:51–56). The girl is seen to be "asleep" until her spirit returns to her body. The same is true of Lazarus. Jesus says, "Our friend Lazarus has fallen asleep; but I am going there to wake him up" (John 11:11–13). *Sleep*, therefore, describes the separation between spirit and body that takes place at death.

11. For a fuller outline of these stages, see Michael Mitton, *The Quick and the Dead*, Pastoral Series, no. 32 (Nottingham, England: Grove Books, 1987).

12. Quoted in Alan Wilkinson, *The Church of England and the First World War* (London: SPCK, 1978), 175.

13. Ibid., 177.

14. Full text of the prayer is in G. K. A. Bell, *Randall Davidson* (Oxford: Oxford University Press, 1938), 828–29.

Chapter 4: Hurtings and Hauntings

1. Michael Perry, ed., *Deliverance* (London: SPCK, 1987), 38.

2. Raphael Gasson, *The Challenging Counterfeit* (Plainfield, N.J.: Logos International, 1968), 33.

3. Kenneth McAll, *Healing the Haunted* (London: Darley Anderson, 1989), 38.

4. Perry, 38–39.

5. J. B. Phillips, *Ring of Truth* (London: Hodder & Stoughton, 1985). See chapter 2.

Chapter 5: Healings and Requiems

1. John Wesley, "A Second Letter to the Author of The Enthusiasm of Methodists and Papists Compared," quoted in E. R. Hardy, "The Blessed Dead in Anglican Piety," *Sobornost* 3, no. 2 (1981): 179–91.

2. While being a pioneer for this approach to ministry, Dr. McAll was by no means alone. Within the Church of England he encouraged and shared in the work of Neil Broadbent, who is based in Derby, and also Robert Law, who is the Bishop of Truro's adviser on the ministry of deliverance.

3. From a taped interview with Dr. McAll at Bignell Wood, Hants, September 1988.

4. Leanne Payne, *The Broken Image* (Westchester, Ill.: Crossway Books, 1986).

5. Kenneth McAll, *Healing the Family Tree* (London: Sheldon Press, 1989), 7–9.

6. McAll, taped interview.

7. Kenneth McAll, "The Church's Ministry of Healing and Healing of the Family Tree" (n.p., n.d.), 4.

8. See, for instance: Luke 10:8–16; John 3:16–17; 5:28–30; Ephesians 2:1–7; 2 Thessalonians 1:5–10; Hebrews 9:27; 10:27; 2 Peter 2:4–9; 3:7.

9. McAll, taped interview.

10. We should not be too disturbed at the subject of visions itself. This phenomenon is becoming more and more a feature of healing ministry within the experience of spiritual renewal. The term *vision* is perhaps too sweeping, and so some people prefer to use the term *a picture from God*. Dr. McAll, however, would say that his visionary experience was quite substantial and not merely a subjective or inward perception. He referred to the opening of the tombs, mentioned in Matthew's gospel, as a visualization similar to his own encounters at requiem Eucharists. This is not convincing, as the account in Matthew 27, itself a product of the death and resurrection of Jesus, is not presented as a vision and contains all the hallmarks of a historic encounter of restored life on the Lazarus scale. Dr. McAll and the two associates previously mentioned (see note 2) reported that they had seen, through visions, a number of the deceased for whom they were praying, attending the requiem Eucharists, sometimes accompanied by angels.

11. See Leviticus 16:1–34; 26:39–45; Numbers 15:22–6; Lamentations 5:7.

12. See Exodus 20:5; 34:7–9; Numbers 14:18–20.

13. Raphael Gasson, *The Challenging Counterfeit* (Plainfield, N.J.: Logos International, 1968), 13–14.

14. Russ Parker, *The Occult: Deliverance from Evil* (Downers Grove, Ill.: InterVarsity Press, 1989).

15. Dr. Kurt Koch, *Christian Counseling and Occultism* (Grand Rapids, Mich.: Kregel, 1972), 307.

16. McAll, *Healing the Family Tree*, 66.

17. Dennis and Matthew Linn with Sheila Fabricant, *Healing the Greatest Hurt* (Mahwah, N.J.: Paulist Press, 1985), 54–55.

Chapter 6: Jesus, the Model for Requiems

1. Used in the Eucharistic Prayer, see *Church of England Common Worship* (London: Church House, 2000). The Sanctus is that part of the Church of England Service that proclaims:

> Holy, holy, holy Lord,
> God of power and might,
> heaven and earth are full of your glory.
> Hosanna in the highest.

2. Ibid., 176f.

Chapter 7: Requiem Healing and Pastoral Care

1. C. S. Lewis, *A Grief Observed* (London: Faber, 1961), 22.

2. A. Plass, *The Growing Up Pains of Adrian Plass* (London: Marshall Pickering, 1986), 100.

3. Bob Jackson, *Matthew* (Guildford: Highland, 1987), 42, 45.

4. John Wimber, *Power Healing* (London: Hodder & Stoughton Religious Division, 1986), 174.

5. *Church of England Common Worship,* Pastoral Services, 345ff.

Chapter 8: Remembering and Releasing

1. Two other versions of this prayer can be found in *Church of England Common Worship,* Pastoral Services, 376.

2. Ibid., 350ff.

Conclusion

1. "Friday Night Live," Central Television, 5 October 1990.

2. Sheldon Vanauken, *A Severe Mercy* (London: Hodder & Stoughton, 1970), 226ff.

3. Ibid., 232.

4. *The Independent*, 22 January 1988, 16.

5. Matthew 17:20–21; see also Luke 17:6 where the same instructions are given with regard to uprooting the mulberry tree.

6. *The Independent*, 16.

The Reverend Michael Mitton works for the Diocese of Derby and is the non-stipendiary vicar of St. Paul's Church, Chester Green, Derby, England. He spent eleven years in parish ministry, directed Anglican Renewal Ministries (encouraging charismatic renewal in the Church of England), edited the magazine *Anglicans for Renewal* and was deputy director of the Acorn Christian Foundation. He also oversaw Christian Listeners in the U.K. and also in Ireland (an ecumenical work nurturing the development of listening skills, particularly as a basis for reconciliation) and Christian Listeners in four centers in South Africa.

Michael has written a number of books, including *The Sounds of God, Restoring the Woven Cord, Wild Beasts and Angels* and *A Heart to Listen*. He is editor of *The Way of Renewal,* a report on renewal for the Church of England Board of Mission, and coauthor with Russ Parker of the workbook for *Healing Wounded History.*

Michael and his wife, Julia, have three children and one grandchild.

The Reverend Dr. Russ Parker is director of the Acorn Christian Foundation, a teaching and training resource for the ministry of Christian healing to the mainstream churches. An ordained Anglican priest with a master's in theology from the University of Nottingham and a doctor of divinity from Columbia (Washington) Evangelical Seminary, he lectured in pastoral care at St. John's College in Nottingham, founded and directed Christian Care and Counsel (now Haven Christian Counselling Centre) and has worked as a facilitator for reconciliation in Northern Ireland and the Republic of Ireland, where he is cofounder and trustee/director of the Christian Training Institute. Russ is also chairman of the Fellowship of Christ the Healer, an association of more than one hundred Christian healing centers.

A few of his books include *Dream Stories, Healing Wounded History, The Wild Spirit, Forgiveness Is Healing, Free to Fail, The Occult, Healing Dreams, Failure* and *Dreams and Spirituality.*

Russ has two adult children and lives with his wife, Roz, in Hampshire, England.